WE MAKE
BEER

Center Point
Large Print

**This Large Print Book carries the
Seal of Approval of N.A.V.H.**

★ SEAN LEWIS ★

WE MAKE BEER

INSIDE THE SPIRIT AND ARTISTRY OF AMERICA'S CRAFT BREWERS

CENTER POINT LARGE PRINT
THORNDIKE, MAINE

ISBN: 978-1-62899-364-6

Library of Congress Cataloging-in-Publication Data

Lewis, Sean, author.
We make beer : inside the spirit and artistry of America's craft brewers /
Sean Lewis. — Center Point Large Print ed.
  pages cm
  Originally published: New York : St. Martin's Press, ©2014.
  ISBN 978-1-62899-364-6 (library binding : alk. paper)
  1. Beer—United States. 2. Microbreweries—United States.
    3. Large type books. I. Title.
  TP577.L486 2014b
  663′.42—dc23
                                                        2014033382

CONTENTS

★ INTRODUCTION ★

"WE'RE MAKING BEER, MAN"

THE TAO OF BEER

I pulled into the parking lot outside of a nondescript set of manufacturing condos. To get there in time, I had woken up early to make the thirty-five-minute commute from my apartment in Boston. I put on a ratty pair of old jeans, the hem of which had long ago frayed from wear, and what hadn't been destroyed by the bottom of my shoes I had evened out with scissors. Stains from spilled beer covered the legs. Soon I would be standing over steaming water and humping heavy bags of grain over my shoulder, but at that moment I was still tired from my job as a sportswriter, farther down the Massachusetts coast, which kept me working well past midnight. After my shift in the brewhouse, I would change into nicer jeans and a polo shirt in my car before heading off to work for the evening. In my hands I carried my brown rubber boots and a few beers I brewed in my kitchen. The boots were sticky and had stray pieces of grain glued to the sides. The brews were for Andris—it was always nice to hear what a professional thought of my work.

I walked in the front door next to the round,

wooden sign that read BLUE HILLS BREWERY, through the little tasting room and gift shop, and into the brewhouse in the rear. Andris was on a ladder near the back checking the temperature in the hot water tank—steam rose from the panel as he lifted it.

"Hey man," he said, always somewhat surprised that I'd made it out of bed. "Good to see you. We're just about ready to mash in. I need ten bags of two-row, four bags of Munich malt . . ." Andris trailed off while listing the grain that would be combined with hot water in order to extract sugars in a process known as the mash. I pulled my boots on and got to work. It was time to make beer.

I met Andris Veidis on a brewery tour. At the time, I was scraping and clawing for every writing assignment I could get to pay the rent on my apartment and put gas in my car. I had written a couple of freelance pieces for *BeerAdvocate* magazine, which had started a new segment called "From the Source" that profiled breweries each month. I was pitching the editors ideas and working as one of the magazine's many freelance contributors. I pitched the idea of a "From the Source" on Blue Hills—it was barely an infant of a brewery, just a few months old, and could provide an interesting perspective on what it took to get started in the industry. Todd Alström, *BeerAdvocate*'s cofounder and the magazine's editor at the time, must have liked the idea because I got the assignment, and so I drove down to Canton, Massachusetts, for the interview.

Andris knew I wasn't bringing a photographer with me, and he dressed the part. His hair looked as though he had just pulled a sweater over his head. He wore cutoff jean shorts and a T-shirt—it was my first glimpse of the brewer's uniform. Most of the conversation centered on the process of building a business and what it took to get a small brewery up and running, but we also spoke about his philosophy of making beer.

"I don't want to make an IPA that is just going to hit you in the face with Cascade hops," he told me—referring to the popular hop grown in the Pacific Northwest that lends a strong grapefruit aroma and flavor to a beer. "Everybody is making those, and they make them because it's really easy. I want my IPA to be more balanced. I want people to drink my beer and say 'Mmm, I've never had an IPA like this before.' "

The best part about writing about beer and breweries was the tasting, and I had a pint of Andris's India pale ale in my hand as we spoke. The hops were present in the nose and first sip, but they did not leap out of the glass and overwhelm. They were subtle and inviting. Alongside the hops, which were more floral than fruity, were a caramel sweetness and a hint of butterscotch.

"That's the diacetyl," Andris explained. "A lot

of people think of it as an off flavor, but I like it. I leave it in there on purpose."

Later I learned that he encouraged the yeast to produce diacetyl by controlling the fermentation temperature and giving the beer time to rest at temperatures slightly lower than that at which it had fermented. Many people never even noticed the subtle flavor behind the strong caramel notes, and others would confuse it with oxidation—said to taste like wet cardboard—a mistake that Andris seemed to take personally.

"I had this beer snob give me an appraisal of my beer at one of my first accounts. He sipped it, sort of swirled it around a bit and sniffed it and looked like a total jackass." Andris imitated the appraiser, tilted his head back, pursed his lips, and swirled around an imaginary glass of IPA. "He said, 'The hops are weak, and I detect a hint of oxidation.' I know what oxidation tastes like, and my IPA did not taste like a lunch bag. It tastes just how I want it to taste. I can't get upset if this guy is just a snob who thinks he knows more than he does."

After the interview, I told him that one day I would like to have a brewery of my own, and that I'd love to learn how a full-scale brewery works firsthand. His response surprised me.

"Bring some boots, because you're going to get wet."

The next brew session was a few days away, so I bought a pair of dairy boots on my way to my newspaper job and dug out an old pair of jeans from the back of my closet. I barely slept the night before, thanks in part to a long Red Sox and Yankees game that delayed the sports section but also because of the anticipation of the next morning.

When I arrived for that first brew session, the building appeared empty. Steam rose from the hot water tank, but the rest of the brewery remained still. I walked toward the kettle, afraid to touch anything. It all seemed so foreign and liable to spew boiling water with the flip of a switch. Finally, Andris emerged from the cold room where the beer rested for a week or two after it was filtered. "Oh," he said, "you made it. Good."

"What are we brewing today?" I asked as we shook hands.

"Xtra Pale, but just half a batch. See that stack of grain over there? I need ten bags of pale malt and one bag of Munich. Bring them over and set them up on the platform next to the mash tun."

He pointed to the pallet loaded with grain bags and then to the mash tun where they would be emptied and their contents soaked in hot water to extract the sugar. My anxiety about brewing was already put to rest. Lift and tote—I could do that. The Xtra Pale Ale was Blue Hills' lightest beer. It was crisp and had a nice floral smell and taste that meshed well with the semisweet finish. The beer was a big hit with the Bud Light crowd that didn't expect much flavor in its beer. It also meant that I would not have to lift as many bags of grain as I would if we were making the more robust IPA.

Next, Andris showed me how to control the flow of hot and cold water into the tun—in this case, a twenty-barrel (620-gallon) steel tank with a hatch on the top to add the grain, a hatch on the side to remove it, and a false bottom to allow the sugary runoff to be pumped out of the tun and into the kettle. It was critical to hit the right temperature so that the naturally present enzymes in the grain could go about their business of converting starch into sugars that the yeast would then turn to alcohol. As I poured the grain in, Andris made sure I dumped every scrap and kernel into the tank. "Gotta get my money's worth out of every bag," he said. I was slow, and the bags were heavy, and pretty soon we had to slow down the water so I could get in all the grain before the tank was full. It was the work of a rookie, and thankfully Andris was patient, telling me to hit the gym.

As the day progressed, I learned which pumps were necessary to transfer the sugary liquid, called wort (pronounced WURT), from the mash tun to the kettle and from the kettle through the heat exchanger and into the fermentation tank. I learned what a C-clamp was, and I learned that a ball valve and a twist of a lever is all that stood between a clean floor and a floor covered in five hundred gallons of beer. I used a large paddle to scrape all the grain I had dumped into the tun, now three times as heavy and steaming hot, out of the mash tun and into fifty-five-gallon plastic buckets. When they were full, I dragged the buckets to the loading dock, where they waited for a local dairy farmer to take them to feed his stock.

I learned the terminology and methods of the brewery. I learned about the vorlauf (VOR-loff), the process of recycling wort over the grain bed to establish a natural filtration system. This helped limit the amount of protein that made its way into the kettle, and when that process was bogged down by clumps of grain in the drains, I watched Andris attach a hose to pump in water and dislodge the clog. I scrubbed more tanks, and I learned how to use the portable pump with buckets of iodine and caustic chemicals to clean and sanitize.

I worked for free, and Andris rewarded my efforts with plenty of beer, a grilled burger on brew days, and conversation. Although there was a small sales staff and a handful of others around the building, it was typically just me and Andris in the brewhouse. Eventually, I could run a brew day by myself, and did so on one occasion, when a hops shipment didn't arrive in the morning and Andris had to drive down the Cape to buy some off another brewery.

I discovered, through my apprenticeship and in talking with brewers across the country, that there is much more to the art of brewing than simple, mechanical beer making. There is, in every brewer I met, a unifying spirit—a Tao, if you will. It is neither a quiet nor a solitary examination of values but a constant dialogue centered on a fundamental desire to satisfy.

"I make beer because I like to drink beer, and so does everybody else," Andris told me once. "I figure if I'm making people happy, then I'm doing something right. And if I can make a buck doing it, then good for me."

It was that simple. There was no grandiose vision of delivering the masses from mass-produced, monotonous beer. Nor was there a desire for great fame or recognition. Andris's approach was based on the notion that somewhere not too far away, somebody would get off work, change into comfortable shoes, grab a beer out of the fridge, and find a moment of satisfaction in that first taste. It might not solve all of life's problems, but when he or she took that first drink, everything would be made just a little bit lighter, a bit better. People depend on brewers to provide them with that moment of relief, and brewers take their role in that relationship seriously.

Like everything learned in the brewhouse, I discovered the Tao of the brewmaster with beads of sweat on my brow. While I shoveled hundreds of pounds of semisweet, sticky grains from the mash tun into farm-bound barrels, Andris and I found time to talk. The physical labor was strenuous but required little conscious thought, which left room for plenty of conversation between labored breaths. Mainly, we talked about beer—new recipe ideas, ideal mash temperatures, fermentation schedules, and tweaks to old recipes. Andris and Blue Hills' other owners are Latvian, and I encouraged him to brew a Baltic porter.

"I think if you brew something that would be unique to Blue Hills, especially something that you could provide a great background story for, I think people would eat that up," I said.

Andris wasn't as enthusiastic. "I don't want to just brew something because it is brewed where I am from," he told me. "I want to do something different, something that you can't find on shelves everywhere. What do you think about an imperial red ale?" The term "imperial" was used originally to denote a beer brewed for the Russian imperial court, when the czars still ruled, and it came to be associated with strong stouts. However, modern brewers attach the "imperial" moniker to any beer that is double the strength of the standard version of their beer.

"Imperial IPAs are real popular right now," I suggested. "I think an imperial red could work nicely."

And so, like that, Blue Hills imperial red IPA was born. Andris would eventually follow it with a beer similar to a Baltic porter, his Black Hops, released later that year. Like a Baltic porter, it gave off some spicy and dark fruit flavors that went well with the roasted and chocolate malts. It was brewed with German malts, as opposed to the English malts that dominate traditional porters. His Black Hops also had a larger-than-usual proportion of hops—offering a less smooth fusion of flavors than in the IPA, with the hops and malt standing in a sort of contradiction with each other. But it was what Andris had wanted—a beer that could stand on a shelf next to an English porter, a Baltic porter, an IPA, or a black IPA and yet retain its distinctive character. Also, it was delicious.

I admired that Andris was unafraid to try something new and unique. He wasn't trying to do something different for its own sake. He was always looking to add his imprint to the marketplace. Occasionally I brought in a bottle of my home brew or a commercial beer that had blown me away, and even if it wasn't in line with his tastes, he would take a moment to think about it. "When I drink other beer, I'm trying to figure out what I like about it and what I would do differently."

Andris was pragmatic. He didn't have to like Baltic porter to understand why I did. He was open-minded. Anyone willing to put in the effort to help him make beer was fine by him: "All I need to know is if he is going to make it easier or harder for me to run my business."

I liked to think that I was fairly pragmatic as well. But I had an unhealthy tendency toward obsession. As a journalist, I constantly fought to keep the sports section error-free. But when I was visibly frustrated trying to keep the mash at the right temperature, Andris laughed and told me to relax: "We're making beer, man!"

As a home brewer, I was meticulous with my notes and measurements. I followed formulas in Ray Daniels's *Designing Great Beers* as if they'd been written on stone tablets and carried down from Mount Sinai, and I used computer software to double-check my calculations and keep track of my recipes. And yet my beer never quite came out the way I'd hoped. Sometimes I missed my mash temperature. Sometimes I collected too much run-off. Something seemed to go wrong with each batch. The beer tasted good, sometimes great; but it was never perfect because I always knew that mistakes had been made. When Andris told me to relax, that we were just making beer, it took a moment to process.

"I'm not trying to say that it isn't important to have a good recipe or a good plan for your beer," he explained. "But what really matters is what it tastes like. Nobody is going to look at your notes, see that you missed your projected original gravity [the measure of sugar dissolved in the wort], and then declare that it's a terrible beer because of that. It doesn't matter how many IBUs [International Bittering Units] your beer has, just how the hops are perceived. I don't even measure IBU, and I probably wouldn't measure gravity if it wasn't necessary to track fermentation. All that matters," he said, "is the final product."

Beer geeks can find faults in any beer. But nobody was going to sample his Xtra Pale Ale, for example, and conclude that the mash temperature had drifted slightly higher than it should have for a couple of minutes. As long as he—and I—could adapt to the complications that arose, everything would be fine. But this did not translate to carelessness or inattention.

When problems arose, Andris addressed them. One week, a couple of his new accounts complained that the beer was flat and wouldn't keep a head—the frothy foam that tops each pint. In order to fix the problem, Andris set about tweaking the recipe to introduce more head-retaining proteins.

Those minor quirks and missteps meant that each batch was unique. We never tried to do two batches exactly the same, because Andris was constantly tweaking the recipes as the brewery grew. When he felt his beer was a little too dry, he changed the mash temperature. He added more hops when he thought his IPA was too sweet. As we continued to experiment with minor adjustments, it began to sink in: *We're making beer*. Blue Hills, like small breweries all over the country, is not a fully automated operation. The human presence meant that mistakes could and would be made. But it also meant that the beer was the result of somebody's craftsmanship. And that human quality, the kind of imprecision that initially chafed against my own need for absolute control, was, I came to realize, precisely what made the beer special.

I chalked Andris's easygoing nature up to personal idiosyncrasy. But as I interviewed brewers across the country for my monthly column, the same attitude emerged again and again. They were generous and honest and saw life much differently than I—or any of my colleagues at the paper—did. Across the country, brewers shared the same thoughts on subjects like collaboration, tradition, innovation, and improvisation.

But what they shared most was captured in a sentence I heard over and over again: "I love my job."

The more I heard others say it, the more I realized that I did not love my job. I did not love eating dinners in my car or at my desk. I did not love fighting to move up in a struggling industry in the midst of a major transformation. And I did not love seeing the faces of the local football coaches more than I did my own girlfriend's. So, I made some changes. I got engaged, I quit my job, and I went back to school for my master's degree. I got married, and my wife and I made plans to move back to California after graduation.

When the time came to move, neither my wife nor I wanted to say good-bye to our friends from the East, but we both wanted to return to California. My twin brother, Steven, planned to fly out to keep me company on the drive west, as Victoria flew home early in order to prepare for and take the California bar exam. I rented a large U-Haul truck with a trailer to tow our car and made loose plans for the trip. The only thing I knew for certain was that Steve and I were going to stop at brewpubs along the way so that we could taste the flavors of every region. Days before my departure, I felt apprehensive about the changes ahead.

I returned to my friend Andris one last time. By then, he had a new volunteer assistant, whom he'd left in charge while we shared a pint of IPA. Again, I asked him what it took to get started. I knew what it took to launch a brewery, since that was the subject of my article on Blue Hills a year prior. What I wanted to know was what it took *from him*. What sacrifices had he made? Did he have a backup plan? What would he do if he failed?

He thought about my questions for a second. I was used to his playful jokes, and so the sincerity of his answer stuck with me.

"When I was trying to decide if I wanted to do

this all out or not, my uncle gave me some advice. He told me that whether I succeeded or failed in this business, I was going to be happy I tried. People go their whole lives and do something that they hate just to pay the bills, but it takes balls to do something you love even though you don't know that you're going to make money. He told me, 'If you do this, you'll have the biggest balls on the block.'

"Even if the business failed, it wouldn't mean that I had failed," he continued. "I never thought that I was going to go out and tank right from the start, but even if I did, my uncle still had a point. It's not just about knowing what you want, it's about having the balls to try and get it."

When we met, I was a reporter, a way for Andris to build some press for his nascent brewery. But we spoke now as friends. He admitted to hardships—he had yet to see much financial reward from his venture.

"The good thing is that I don't have to spend any more money on beer. The bad thing is that I don't really have any money to spend on beer." It was good to see that his sense of humor remained intact.

Andris felt the sting from his sacrifices, but I also sensed that he was happy. He was happy because his uncle was right, and he was happy because the business seemed poised to grow and take off any day. In fact, about a year after that conversation, Andris sent me a picture message of the brewery's fourth fermentation vessel being installed. It was the second upgrade and minor expansion in the brewery's history.

In order to make sure that happened, Andris was doing everything it took to build Blue Hills.

"I brought a keg of Watermelon Wheat to a family party the other weekend." Neither he nor I was the biggest fan of the fruity beer, but it was always popular at beer fests and in the bars during the summer. "My brother was drinking some of it, and he said, 'I can't believe you're selling out with a fruit beer.' But it's one of my most popular beers. What am I supposed to do? I told him, 'I'm not selling out; I'm selling beer.' And you know what? It was a hot day, and that was a damn nice beer to be drinking outside with my family."

We shook hands and wished each other luck, but not before he sent me off with enough beer to fill the trunk of my car and a growler each of his Spring Märzen and India pale ale.

"This ought to help you bribe some people to help you load your truck, and a little more for you to enjoy when you get home. You'll be the only guy in California with Blue Hills beer."

I left the brewery a day before I would pack all of my things into the U-Haul and two days before I planned on saying farewell to Boston. My friend impressed me with his gumption, and I knew from my conversations with other brewers that he was not the only brewer from whom I could learn.

★ 1 ★

"I SEE CREATING AND INVENTING AS PART OF BEER'S TRADITION"

OLD-WORLD TRADITION AND NEW-WORLD INNOVATION

Two photos hang on the wall in Matt Brynildson's office. One Matt took himself; the other is hundreds of years old. They show, essentially, the same thing. Rows upon rows of barrels stacked on themselves with tubes and troughs connecting them. The photos are dark and dimly lit. They are depictions of an English style of fermentation vessels known as union barrels —the old one was taken in the sixteenth century at an old Bass brewing facility, the other in the twenty-first century at Marston's Burton upon Trent brewery. They illustrate the way the tools of the brewer have not changed in hundreds of years. The mystique of the old-world brewing process emanates from behind the framed glass.

Not far from these photos in Matt's office, his own stack of barrels rests on the first floor of the Firestone Walker brewery in Paso Robles, California, where Matt makes his living as the award-winning brewmaster. The size and scope of the union barrel system at Firestone Walker is much smaller than in either of the photos, and it's easy enough to move it out of the way when other operations need more space, but the principle behind it remains the same.

When Matt joined Firestone Walker in 2001, the brewery had yet to become the regional power and world-renowned company it is today. Founded by brothers-in-law Adam Firestone and David Walker, the young brewery had been rumored to be fermenting its beer in oak barrels—a process that seemed to their new brewmaster to be overwhelmingly risky and unnecessary.

"When you come to work for Firestone the first thing you learn about is the barrels," Matt said, as he recalled one of his early conversations with Adam Firestone. "And when I came it was in a transitional period when we were moving from one small brewery to this one. My first question was, 'We're not really going to do the barrels, right? That's all smoke and mirrors and marketing. It has nothing to do with how you make your actual beer.'

"And they were like, 'No, it's how we make our actual beer.' 'Yeah, but when you move into the new brewery it's not going to be your focus, right? We're going to do traditional stainless steel?' 'It's nonnegotiable. Ferment in oak.'"

Firestone Walker's dedication to fermenting in oak seems at first glance to be a nod to the traditional English systems of wood-barrel fermentation. After all, David Walker is a Brit himself. But it's not that at all; the story of those barrels is more a comedy of errors than any attempt to preserve tradition.

Both David Walker and Adam Firestone had deep ties to the wine industry. For many outside the beer industry, the Firestone name conjures up images of car tires and vineyards, and right-fully so. The family's beer tradition begins with Firestone Walker, a partnership forged when David married Adam's sister. With their roots in wine and a growing appreciation for beer, Adam and David decided to open a brewery and ferment beer in the used chardonnay barrels that the Firestone winery no longer needed. They tapped Jeffers Richardson to be Firestone Walker's first brewmaster and tasked him with finding a way to make their unique idea work.

"They weren't afraid of oak, but what they didn't realize was [the process] probably wasn't a good fit for beer," said Jeffers, who was eventually replaced by Matt at the helm but has since returned to head up a new barrel-aging program and taproom at Firestone Walker, known as The Barrelworks. "There was a reason why we weren't using that [process]. They wanted to use old wine barrels. They thought that would be great. We could reuse all these old chardonnay barrels. And at the time it resulted in what could only be deemed as disastrous results. This is before you could even dream of making sour beers, let alone by accident."*

Matt wasn't around during this period, but he likened the finished product to "poor salad dressing—malt vinegar at best."

Jeffers did his best to convince Adam and David that fermenting in oak was a bad idea, but they were adamant.

"I kept saying we can't do this, we can't do this, and they said, 'Figure out a way to do it.'"

What Jeffers came up with was the union barrel system. It is an old process developed in England and made popular by original pale ale brewers like Bass. Tubes and hoses connect rows of barrels to one another with a swan-neck pipe coming out of the barrels and into a trough to collect any excess blowoff. Wort, or unfermented beer, is pumped out of the kettle and into these barrels, which fill simultaneously thanks to the connections—hence the name, union. Yeast is added and fermentation takes place. If the carbon dioxide created by the fermentation spews young beer out the blowoff

_____

*Sour beers are popular today but would have died the slow death of neglect on store shelves when Firestone Walker was young. Perhaps a brewery with a strong marketing arm could have had some success in selling a sour style (Berliner Weisse, gueuze, Flanders red, etc.), but if a brewery made sour beers by accident, as Firestone Walker was doing, there was no chance it could sell.

pipe, it is recirculated back into the fermenting beer to save money, since British brewers, unlike brewers in the United States, are taxed on the amount of raw ingredients used, not on the finished product. However, the process dates back well before the era of centralized government and uniform taxation.

"Brewers in Burton upon Trent, they say that the original process was developed by the monks in the area," Matt said. "They found that barrel fermentation afforded them a clearer beer than if they fermented in vats or other vessels. There's something about the shape of the barrel, the surface area of the barrel, or perhaps the wood. There's not an exact science behind it."

At Firestone, the barrels aren't connected to one another the way they are in a true union barrel system, and Matt doesn't harvest the yeast that blows out of the fermentation vessels the way the Brits do. But Firestone Walker managed to learn from the old pale ale brewers in England. Instead of using wine barrels, which can become perfect breeding grounds for undesirable micro-organisms, the Firestone Walker union system is made up of fresh oak barrels that receive a good toasting before being put to use. Only a handful of their beers ever see time in the union system, the most popular of which is the flagship Double Barrel Ale.

The beer begins the fermentation process in a

stainless steel tank, where Matt and his brewing team can control the temperature during the most crucial stages and ensure that the beer begins its life in sanitary conditions. Then, the beer is pumped into the barrels: A hose goes into the barrel, beer is pumped in, and right when it gets to the top a brewer pulls out the hose and jams a bung in its place—then it's on to the next one. When it's done, the brewers stand back and let the yeast do its job. There are no glycol jackets or special temperature-controlled rooms to control the fermentation—just oak and yeast.

"Most brewers look at that as pretty archaic and simplistic, and maybe a little out of control," Matt said. "And it's funny. Paso gets up to 110 degrees in the summer and all the way down to freezing in the winter. You'd think you'd have these massive fluctuations in flavor and fermentation profiles—and it proves a couple of things: that most flavor development in normal ales as we know it from this standpoint is happening in the first twenty-four hours, when we're controlling temperature, and that wood has an incredible insulative character. And it also has a pretty resilient, protective character. Whether it's through tannins or whatever it's through, but it protects that beer from microbiological spoilage. We literally have no or very few spoilers that affect these beers."

After several days in the barrels, the beer is

pumped back into a stainless steel tank and eventually constitutes only about 20 percent of a full batch. The rest of the beer spends its entire fermentation cycle in steel tanks. After it is allowed more time to mature, or condition, the beer is filtered, carbonated, and bottled.

Double Barrel Ale is made in the spirit of traditional English pale ales and doesn't share the kind of brash hop characteristics of Sierra Nevada's iconic pale ale, or even Firestone Walker's own Pale 31. What it does have is a rich caramel and toffee base that balances out the more dramatic hop flavors. Behind that, there is the slightest hint of oak. It doesn't dominate the flavor profile, but it presents itself as nearly an after-thought. It is almost as though you were drinking beer from a wooden cup, and, in your thirst, your tongue accidentally brushed along the rim.

Drinking Double Barrel Ale is a pleasant experience because the beer is refined and easy. However, at the brewery itself, visitors can taste an unfiltered version of the beer. Unlike the version that is bottled and distributed to bars and liquor stores around the country, the unfiltered DBA is something of a daring beer and is fermented entirely in oak. For an unfiltered beer, it is surprisingly clear, with just a slight haze. Unlike the standard version, the oak is present in the nose, as are a slight fruitiness and bits of spice. Whereas DBA is a great beer that graciously recedes into the background of a conversation or a meal, the unfiltered version demands to be the center of attention. It's one of the most popular beers at the Paso Robles tasting room, and for good reason. The beer stands as a prime example of traditional methods employed to make a fantastic product—even if the rest of the brewery is state of the art.

Next door to Matt's office sits the control room for Firestone Walker's brand-new brewing system. It is a Spartan room with little more than a couple of computer monitors on a desk, their screens displaying readouts and charts tracking temperatures and other measurements at virtually every point from the mash tun to the heat exchanger. With the exception of adding hops, every step of the brewing process is automated and controlled by a computer program called BrewMax. Any sort of mystic notions of what working in a full-scale brewery might be like are dispelled at the sight of the screen with its blinking lights, temperature readings, and pH levels on display.

"I think that the brewhouse itself in a brewery is highly overromanticized as having this huge operator-driven impact on the flavor of the product," Matt said. "Wort production, to be honest with you, especially in a production brewery, is super rhythmic. It's super repetitive.

"I mean we will do literally fifty turns through

the brewhouse. The guy who is on the brewhouse is making these repetitive steps throughout the process. Yeah, he's controlling everything and he's monitoring it all—and I think what we've done is to use the automation to take care of all the super repetitive types of things that are also super dependent on time and temperature. If a brewer is over here solving a problem and not watching his brewhouse and takes a little more time to do something or misses a temperature because he was busy doing something else, our consistency goes away. We use the tool to do all the repetitive kind of things that could go wrong if you weren't paying attention and should be super easy if you are. He can watch wort quality, he can watch pH, he can watch clarity, and he can use the machine to refine. And he can work faster."

A tour around the brewery revealed an even deeper devotion to modern technology over traditional methods. The few rows of union barrels tucked over to the side of the brewery began to feel less and less significant as Matt showed off the various toys and inventions that make brewing in a modern brewery far simpler than when breweries in Burton upon Trent were pioneering the pale ale.

Virtually all tanks in modern breweries have a long steel tube that comes out of the top and bends downward to about chest height. The opening allows carbon dioxide created during fermentation to escape the tank safely instead of building up toward the point of explosion. At breweries like Blue Hills in Canton, Massachusetts, the brewmaster attaches a short length of hose to the end of this pipe and submerges the other end in a bucket of sanitizer solution. The result is something like an airlock that allows the carbon dioxide to bubble out, often with great vigor, without letting contaminants in. Some breweries only have the one tube coming out of the top, and chemicals are pumped through to clean them when the tank is empty. Inside, usually just a couple inches below the top of the tank, a hollow metal orb resembling a stainless steel whiffle ball is attached to the other end of the tube. This sphere, known as a clean-in-place device, sends chemicals such as caustic wash, acid, or plain hot water spraying out in all directions to clean the tank evenly.

Matt pointed to the top of the steel tubes on his tanks and noted how they were a gentle curve rather than steep right angles going straight into the tank.

"It's a swooping arm with no sharp angles," he said. "That's so we can use the hop cannon."

The practice of dry-hopping, or adding hops to a beer after it has fermented in order to increase hop aroma, is an old one. Brewers have aged their beer on hops, be it in open vats or wooden casks, for about as long as they have been brewing with hops. Until recently, the standard method in most modern breweries has been to add hops to a conditioning tank then pump the fermented beer into that tank—or to open a hatch on top of the tank and dump the hops in. The hop cannon allows brewers to pump the fermenting beer through the device, which is filled with aroma hops, and back into the tank, thus eliminating the need for a secondary vessel. It also allows greater control of the dry-hopping process, since brewers are able to add hops on different days, to add a layer of complexity to the beer's aroma.

"The swooping arm lets the hops flow in freely without getting jammed up like they would if there were right angles," Matt said. His face beamed as he mimed the action of attaching a hop cannon to the tank, like a kid describing a new toy.

The hop cannon and automated brewhouse are undeniably cool. There's a level of technological savvy involved that makes the Firestone Walker brewery feel like one part factory, one part mad scientist laboratory. But that's nothing compared with what's just across the narrow hallway from Matt's office upstairs.

Matt's first job in the beer industry wasn't in a brewery. Matt graduated from Kalamazoo College with a degree in chemistry, which he put to work as a hop chemist for Michigan's Kalsec, Inc., a color, flavor, and nutrient manufacturer for the food industry. He was already an avid home brewer, but his time in the lab working on hop extracts only furthered his appreciation and love for beer. He went back to school, but this time it was brewing school, at the Siebel Institute of Technology, in Chicago. After graduating, he was hired by a then-fledgling brewpub in Chicago called Goose Island, which he helped grow into the well-known brewery that it is today. He made his way out west to San Luis Obispo Brewing Company (SLO Brew) and was eventually hired by Firestone Walker when Adam and David purchased SLO Brew's facility. His chemist roots were partly why he was so flummoxed by Adam and David's insistence on fermenting in oak barrels.

"I've got this quality piece in place," he said. "I know how to control the process in stainless. I'm not that interested in barrel aging from the standpoint of consistency, so I was always kind of pushing back there. And here it is nonnegotiable. You have to ferment in barrels. They always make the point that we ferment in barrels; we don't age in barrels."

Matt's brewing prowess has made him famous throughout the beer community, but the brewmaster never lost sight of his roots in science. Now, his appreciation for good chemistry is the product of a desire for ultimate consistency. The whole purpose behind the automation of the brewhouse, the modern technology, and the state-of-the-art quality-control lab across the tiny hallway from Matt's office is to maintain an optimum level of consistency.

"We take the quality program super seriously," Matt said. "We've got four full-time quality-control technicians. An analytical chemist, a microbiologist, and a sensory technician make up the team as well as a quality manager."

At the moment, the QC guys were out of the lab. They may have been down on the brewery floor, perhaps gathering samples of fermenting beer. Their lab was expectedly clean, with microscopes here, cabinets full of lab equipment over there, and an expensive-looking minifridge up on the counter. Matt opened the door to the fridge to reveal boxes of slides and small vials—samples taken from fermentation tanks and union barrels to be checked for undesirable microbes.

"If you look in here, there are probably as many samples for barrels as there are for fermenters, because every barrel in our union is basically treated like a separate fermenter."

The lab is also where Firestone Walker's microbiologist maintains and tests the various yeast strains used in the brewery's beer. Although it is not uncommon for a brewery to use a single yeast strain for all its beers while adjusting variables such as time and temperature in fermentation to brew certain styles, Firestone Walker maintains at least three at all times: an ale strain, a lager strain, and a Hefeweizen strain.

Quantities of yeast are sampled and examined under a microscope to make sure that they haven't become contaminated by other yeasts—either naturally occurring wild yeasts or any of the other strains used in the brewery. It is this kind of dedication to consistency that provides one of the biggest difference between modern beer and the beer brewed centuries ago.

A beer like Firestone Walker's Pale 31,* named for California's admittance to the United States as the thirty-first state in the union, would suffer greatly from inconsistency. Unlike a porter, characterized by its dark and strong-flavored malts, or the German lagers, whose long aging periods allowed the yeast to steadily clean up unwanted flavors, a new-world beer like Pale 31

------

*Because I write about it, I'm often asked what my favorite beer is. This is an impossible question to answer. It's worse than asking a parent which of his kids is his favorite. I could probably list a dozen beers to put down as my favorite depending on certain conditions such as my favorite beer to drink with pizza, my favorite beer to drink on my patio on a summer day, and so on. However, if I had to choose one beer to drink for the rest of my life, it would be Firestone Walker's Pale 31. It's not necessarily the best beer ever made, and it's not even the most exciting beer in Firestone Walker's lineup, but it is incredibly well balanced, and the flavors are exciting enough without being overwhelming. It's truly a remarkable beer.

demands uniformity in the brewing process. The hop profile is brilliant but delicate. All its floral wonders could easily be overshadowed by a hint of sour apple notes from wild yeast or any number of the myriad off flavors that can develop if fermentation temperatures are allowed to vary beyond the yeast's comfort zone. Similarly, the bright, golden-sweet body of the beer that plays in perfect harmony with the floral hops is wholly dependent on the brewer's ability to mash the grains at the proper temperature. Soaking the grain at the wrong temperature could result in a beer that is too thin or too sweet. Everything has to be just right.

Matt had the chance to brew Pale 31 at Marston's Burton upon Trent facility in England, where the union barrel system was pioneered. He was underwhelmed by the results: "It didn't have the same hop impact that we look for. Our dry-hopping methods here are much more refined than what they're doing," Matt said. But he did leave the old-world brewery with a better understanding of the roots of the union barrel system and how modern British breweries operate them today.

Most surprising to him was Marston's lack of laboratory testing on the barrels in the union. Unlike at Firestone Walker, where each barrel is tested several times to ensure freedom from undesirable microbes, there was an assumed level of contamination in the barrels at Marston's facility,* according to Matt. Matt also explained that Marston's use of the union barrels was more functional than Firestone Walker's—a means of harvesting yeast at its most active point (as opposed to after fermentation is completed, as many American brewers practice). At Firestone Walker, the union barrels are intended to affect the flavor of the beer inside, whereas at Marston's the barrels are used simply as fermentation vessels and a way to harvest yeast. "They're using neutral oak, they're using well-exhausted oak, so they're not getting any oak impact at all—in fact they don't want that. They consider that an off flavor. In our union, we are trying to get the oak flavor into the beer—that's why we're doing it.

"We both do the same process, but we're doing it for completely different reasons. Any yeast that comes out of the union is discarded in our program; any yeast that comes out of their union

_____

*This is not to say that the brewers at Marston's are producing beer that is contaminated or that will make consumers sick. No known pathogens can survive in beer. In addition, the "assumed level of contamination" to which Matt is referring would most likely never spoil a batch of beer, as active fermentation deters bacteria and wild yeasts from taking over. At the worst, a small level of contamination would mean less consistency between batches.

is captured, and that's what's used to pitch everything else in the brewery. They use the union for yeast propagation, and we're using it for flavor development."

So, what's the right way to do it? The pioneers of pale ale don't bother checking their numerous oak barrels for contamination, so should Firestone Walker really be concerned? Isn't there wisdom in the methods of the old-world brewers? The United Kingdom's Campaign for Real Ale, or CAMRA, seems to think so.

Real ale, or unfiltered, unpasteurized ale served out of a cask through traditional hand pumps or by simple gravity, used to be the standard form of ale in the British Isles for centuries. However, as modern technology was able to turn beer into an über-consistent commodity in steel kegs, real ale started to disappear from the British beer scene. But in the late 1970s, CAMRA began its crusade toward bringing beer in Britain back to its roots and away from the mass-produced swill that had taken over the pubs.

But America isn't Great Britain. American brewers didn't have the same resources as those of their parent country, so they improvised. Molasses was a popular ingredient in colonial-era brews, as were many other items that would make a devotee of Reinheitsgebot (the German purity laws) blow steam out his ears.

"One of the traditions, to me, of brewing is innovation," said Jim Koch. As the founder of Boston Beer Company, maker of Samuel Adams, Koch is better qualified than most to speak on the subject. "I see creating and inventing as part of beer's tradition. My dad had a brewing patent, my grandfather had a brewing patent; I have several. So, to me, again this is sort of a lived experience for me—you read about it in a book and you think, 'Oh, I need to respect brewing tradition.' If you actually grew up among brewers, you realize they have always been innovative, at least here in the United States, and that's my family's tradition. Innovating, pushing boundaries and doing new things—just approaching everything with a questioning attitude, that to me is part of the tradition of American brewing. I don't find a dichotomy there. I know my dad didn't, and I know my grandfather didn't."

Few American brewers can stand next to Jim and claim to have comparable brewing credentials. Take away the fact that he founded Sam Adams in the 1980s, when there were essentially no options apart from mass-produced American lagers and imported German lagers, take away the fact that his brewery survived through a boom and bust phase of microbreweries during the 1990s and grew to be the largest craft brewery in the United States, and Jim still has his remarkable brewing pedigree. The recipe that eventually became his flagship Boston Lager came from his great-great-grandfather.

"It sort of made me unique within craft brewing to have six generations of history in brewing, and not as owners but as brewmasters," he said. "It was not even a business tradition; it was the brewmaster's tradition. That's unique in American craft brewing. It gave me a deep sense of history—not just read but lived. My father's friends were brewers. My grandfather's friends were brewers. I remember them as a kid. Some of them were quite colorful. It gave me a very deep, historical respect for the traditions and the sort of art of brewing."

As Jim is fond of saying, his roots and love for brewing did not come from reading books, but from family experience. The result of those generations is a company that often suffers attacks in the form of carping on Internet forums that accuse Sam Adams of outgrowing its roots and putting profits ahead of product. But these criticisms often miss the point entirely. Named for an American patriot instrumental in the American Revolution, the Boston Beer Company and the Sam Adams brand have been instrumental in the American beer revolution. To be sure, Sam Adams the beer is not the only founding father of the new United States of Beer, just as the original Samuel Adams wasn't the only founding father of the United States of America. But Adams had a knack for inspiring those around him to join the cause, and Sam Adams frequently serves as a gateway to better beer for the college-age drinkers who previously believed that beer was best served in plastic cups on a Ping-Pong table or straight from the keg with one's legs held above one's head. It was the occasional six-pack of Boston Lager in college that led me to a realization that beer could be enjoyed as an end in itself, rather than a means toward getting blackout drunk.

Sam Adams provided me—and surely others—with my road to Damascus moment, in terms of enjoying beer. Perhaps the biggest contribution the brewery has given the American beer scene, apart from its offering an example of virtually every style of beer (at the time of this writing, the Sam Adams Web site listed sixty-four beers ranging in style from Vienna Lager to Maple Pecan Porter to Belgian IPA), is the way it has, for many, become the new face of American beer. In many ways, the Boston Beer Company has become the standard bearer of beer culture in America. Sometimes, the company stands at the vanguard of the culture, and other times it catches up to the trends (despite its wide array of styles, Sam Adams seemingly took forever to release an IPA). Its position as a leader or a follower may be up for debate, but its participation in defining beer culture in the United States is clear—even if beer's role in American culture is still being determined.

"I guess I can start by saying beer is not this monolithic thing," Jim said. "It's like saying, What role does air play in American culture? It's pervasive. It is part of not only everyday life but really special occasions among friends and family. And today, the enjoyment of craft beer has become part of people's coming of age in appreciation of food and beverages themselves."

Like a music aficionado seeking out that limited-release album, craft beer culture in America seems to have a fascination with trying new beer after new beer—even to the point of neglecting older classics. On Internet forums, beer drinkers who seek out new beer at the expense of drinking their favorites are known as "tickers." Many of these tickers are blamed for generating hype for rare beers. Even if a beer is of lower quality than a readily available beer from a different brewer, it can become more valuable among beer traders simply because of its rarity.

Similarly, brewers become guilty of putting out limited-release beers that can generate this level of hype and put the brewery's name into the beer-geek world as a desirable brewery. Although Sam Adams is already one of the most recognizable beer brands in America, it too occasionally releases beers for the purpose of doing something newsworthy and interesting rather than simply making a good beer. At least, this was the perception of Samuel Adams's Infinium.

Infinium was first released in the winter of 2010 as a champagne-like brew. Although the style itself is not new—bières de champagne like DeuS from Brouwerij Bosteels in Belgium have existed long before Infinium—the method used to create the beer was completely original, prompting Samuel Adams to market the beer as something completely new and revolutionary. The key difference in the process takes place during the mash. Instead of soaking the grain in hot water, usually around 152 degrees, for a short time, usually around an hour, Samuel Adams mashed the grain at lower temperatures for much longer—a reported 60–70 degrees for several days. The desired result of this extended and strange mashing process was to extract as much starch and sugar out of the malted grain as possible in order to create a dry and high-alcohol beer without the use of adjuncts like sugar. It was released in the winter as an alternative to champagne for New Year's Eve and holiday parties.

The reception to Infinium was mixed. Some felt that the beer was a syrupy and malty mess with little to no hop presence. Indeed, the noble hops used in the brewing process are faint at best. For those drinkers for whom "quality" really only means "hoppy," Infinium was a complete disaster. Then there were others who wrote the beer off as little more than a gimmick.

Still, the beer represented a remarkable

departure from the standard brewing process and put Samuel Adams back in the conversation with the leaders of experimental brewing. Personally, I liked it. I never treated the beer as something I could pop open after a long day at work as I might another beer. I approached it as I believe it was meant to be approached—as I would a bottle of champagne. I shared it with friends on New Year's Eve, and with family during Christmas dinner. Infinium fizzed like champagne, but had a slightly buttery taste. Although it was dry, it also had a bit more body than standard champagne.

Still, the most remarkable part about the beer was not the end result but the process. The stated goal was to create a high-alcohol, champagne-style beer without breaking any of the rules set forth by the German purity law, or Reinheitsgebot, which essentially states that no beer shall be made with ingredients other than water, malt, hops, and yeast. The radical departure from standard mash practices wasn't an attempt to do something crazy, but an effort to meet the challenge of crafting a very specific beer that would be hard to create without the use of adjuncts. This approach fits well with Samuel Adams, which tries to adhere to tradition when possible but isn't afraid to challenge those traditions when necessary.

"You understand why [tradition is] there, what purpose it accomplishes," Jim said. "The hops that we use in Boston Lager are extremely traditional hops—centuries old. We get them from their original growing areas. Some of the farmers that we deal with, their families have been growing hops on that same land for three hundred years. That's tradition. I've watched for thirty years people trying to improve on those hops—on Hallertau Mittelfruh in particular. There've probably been a dozen substitutes developed that are more disease resistant, higher yield, easier to grow—but they don't taste like Hallertau Mittelfruh.

"In that sense, that's a traditional thing that we're very committed to because it delivers a unique and special flavor, and nobody has duplicated that flavor. If you could improve on it some way, sure. For example, those hops—you need to grow those hops in that terroir, but we noticed over the years that we were selecting hops that other people weren't, and it was because we were selecting them for flavor and aroma and other people were selecting them for physical appearance—were they nice, bright green? Did they not have wind burn? Do they have a certain sheen? There's a certain visual standard for selection of these hops that has been in place for centuries.

"We try to do things not just for tradition but because tradition makes sense. We noticed that there was a negative correlation between the appearance and aroma and taste characteristics of the hops. Long story short: For centuries, the Bavarian hop farmers have been harvesting these hops about a week too early because brewers were selecting them based on physical appearance, which peaked earlier than flavor and aroma. If you left them in the field for an extra week to ten days, while the appearance degraded, the aroma and flavor developed more in the hops. We blew up centuries of German hop-harvesting tradition because we could improve the aroma and flavor of the hops."

It might be possible for some to look at Jim Koch's practice of reconsidering centuries of hop-harvesting tradition as typical American arrogance. Really, who is he and who are his brewers to come to Germany, where hops have been grown for beer for centuries, and tell them that they are doing it wrong? Why should German brewmasters whose families have been crafting pristine lagers using noble hops for as long as their recorded histories go back be persuaded by a Yankee to change their methods? It would be easy to write Jim off as a know-it-all with no respect for the way things have been done, but it would be wrong.

Jim's quest is not to shake out the old cobwebs from the beer world but to continue pushing forward. To do that, he enlisted the oldest member of the old guard. Samuel Adams gets a lot of credit for Infinium, and it often takes a lot of the criticism for that beer as well. But what frequently gets lost in the story of that beer is that it was a collaborative effort with the oldest brewery in the world.

When Jim and his brewing team set out to create a new beer brewed in a completely new manner, it was done alongside the masters from the Weihenstephan brewery. The brewers there in the town of Freising, just outside of Munich, are part of a tradition that dates back to when beer was first brewed at the Weihenstephan Monastery in the eleventh century. It sits atop Naehrberg Hill and is surrounded by the modern Weihenstephan Science Centre for Life and Food Sciences, of the Technical University of Munich, where brewers from around the world come to study brewing science. The site is something of a holy ground for brewers, and its impact was not lost on Jim when he visited the brewery to work with its masters.

"Coming from a brewing family—where one hundred and fifty years is a long time in the U.S.—to be working with a brewery that is a thousand years old, it's just reverential. No brewer can walk up that hill in Freising, where Weihenstephan is, without feeling just reverence for the brewing history," Jim said. "To walk up that hill and think, wow, for one thousand years brewers have walked up this hill to make their beer. That's amazing. That's a very cool thing. This was before the battle of Hastings they were brewing beer there. So, it's hard to really describe that feeling unless you're a brewer.

"I get to be one in a thousand-year chain of brewers. That's unbelievable. For a guy who started twenty-nine years ago and was brewing in his kitchen to be partnering with the oldest brewery in the world—that was just a magical experience."

Ultimately, the fundamentals of brewing traditions in the modern beer world are less rigid than, say, Reinheitsgebot. At the basic level, brewers have been doing the same thing since the first time a sloppy prehistoric Sumerian farmer left grains out in the rain. There are historians far more skilled than I who have worked to add detail to the history of beer, which moves from the Middle Ages, when beer was safer to drink than water, through the age of empires and colonization. Those beer makers have all led us to today, where contemporary brewers continue to convert the sugars extracted from grains into alcohol seasoned and flavored with hops and other ingredients.

The union barrel system at Firestone Walker is not the same as the one employed at Marston's, nor is it very similar to the ones first employed by the first pale ale brewers at Burton upon Trent. But it does provide a romantic link to the past. There are small breweries that pride themselves on their rustic methods, but even they often add modern and experimental twists to their beers. What older methods offer in nostalgia or romance they often lack in the kind of quality control that enables brewers like Matt Brynildson to consistently craft some of the best beer in the world, thus making the use of modern technology and understanding an essential part of the brewing process. Not only does it produce better beer, but it allows Firestone Walker to grow as a company and reach a wider audience that would likely be turned off by an inconsistent product.

It seems as though, when it comes to the tradition of beer, the most important tradition is striving to make better beer. Unlike the ancient traditions of religion, the old processes have never been sanctified. The only thing that matters with beer is the final product. If it tastes good, if it makes people happy, then it's good beer. The beer community often celebrates "doing things the right way." The right way means treating brewing tradition with its due respect, but not so blindly as to ignore opportunities for innovation. Jim Koch does that. So does Matt. They are among the leaders of the American beer revolution, and even as they leave some older brewing methods behind, they keep them ever in sight. Even as practices of the past are passed over, the spirit behind those traditions remains intact—as it has for thousands of years.

★ 2 ★

"THAT MEANS I'M DOING IT RIGHT"

APPRECIATING BALANCE IN BEER AND BREWING

Spend enough time at a bar, and you may start to notice some interesting faces as patrons drink their beer. The man with the Bud Light bottle tips it to his lips, holds for a second, and then brings it back down to the bar. If his face reacts, it's to the game on the screen.

The woman with the Trappist ale takes her first sip. It is slow but measured. Her eyes widen as she tips the goblet to her lips. When she sets it down, she gives the beer another glance, an eyebrow raised, her mouth presenting an approving smirk. Her head bobs slightly as if to agree, "Yes, that's good."

The hophead at the end of the bar with the beard and the brewery T-shirt has had his imperial IPA for a minute and hasn't even taken a sip yet. He holds his pint glass in both hands, trying to get it warmer, and takes whiff after whiff. His face gets so close that he accidentally dips his nose into the beer—an occupational hazard of sniffing with eyes closed. Wiping the beer from his nose, he takes a gulp and a wave washes over his face. The first reaction is a widening of his eyes, followed quickly by a scrunching of his nose and mouth as the bitterness ravages his palate. When it's all down, he works to open his mouth behind lips still trying to hold in the flavor. He lets out a quiet "whoo" that expresses his pleasure. The taste of grapefruit from the Cascades and Amarillo hops still lingers in his mouth, but he needs another minute before his palate is refreshed. He returns to sniffing his foamy glass, then taps out some notes on his smartphone.

And then there is the beer drinker tucked into a corner booth with a group of friends. They laugh and gossip, or perhaps they're carping about work with beers in front of them. This beer drinker did not seek out something simple and forgettable, nor did this beer drinker go for the aggressive flavors that other patrons sought. The beer in front of this beer drinker is balanced. It might be an IPA or pale ale with just enough toffee sweetness to give the beer a few layers of complexity that play off and counteract the bitterness while still allowing the flavorful hops to shine as the rightful stars of the brew. Or, it could be a dry Irish stout, with a hint of acridity from the roasted barley that provides just the right amount of a harsh counterpoint to the sweet and delicately hopped beer in the same way a splash of milk softens a cup of fine espresso.

Like the hophead, this beer drinker smells the beer before sipping, but does not linger there. A longer gulp follows an inquisitive initial sip. The beer drinker's eyes drift off to another place for that brief moment when the beer is somewhere between the lips and throat. As the glass is set gently back on the table, the beer drinker's tongue pokes out to get one more taste off the lips before they open to reveal a quick smile. The stresses of the day's work are slowly washed away, with layers of lacing on the glass standing as tombstones memorializing each of the annoyances from the previous eight hours. There was morning traffic when everyone slowed down to see the wreck on the other side of the road. Gulp. The boss wanted to have a word "as soon as you get a chance." Gulp. The coworker currently sitting across the table couldn't figure out how to access the right files with the new software. Gulp. The boss left at three, but the beer drinker stayed until half-past five to finish that big project before the weekend. Gulp. This beer was all too necessary.

There may be excitement associated with drinking a big, boozy imperial stout aged for months in a bourbon barrel, but that experience is closer to eating a rich chocolate cake after a meal. A child might prefer cake to everything else, but the adult eater knows that dessert is best eaten sparingly. The real satisfaction comes from the way the chef's warm and creamy polenta played perfectly with the roasted veggies and their just-so-sweet glaze.

• • •

At Blue Hills, Andris poured himself a foamy pint of IPA. The pull of the tap handle, protruding from the outer wall of the brewery's cold room, marked the start of a quick break. It was some time around noon on a summer day, and the brewery was hot—even with the big rolling door opened fully in the back. Scrubbing and hosing down the metal grates that compose the false bottom of the mash tun only made it hotter and added moisture to the air, as did the steam-jacketed kettle full of wort warming its way toward a rolling boil.

After pouring off the excess foam and refilling the glass, he took a big, well-deserved drink. His next words were predictable because he said it just about every time he poured himself a drink: "That's a damn fine beer, if I do say so myself."

In fairness to him, it was a damn fine beer—although others might disagree.* Blue Hills IPA is an English-style IPA, but brewed with American ingredients. The end result is, to some, a lot of confusion and disappointment. For example, this

---

*In the early years for Blue Hills, the IPA tasted different out of the bottle than it did on tap. This was due in part to the fact that it was brewed by a contract brewery with a bottling line. Although the same recipe was used, the difference in equipment and minor tweaks in process created a beer that seemed slightly off in bottles.

is an excerpt from a review of the beer as it appeared in *BeerAdvocate* magazine in December 2009:

> Unique, despite the market being flooded with IPAs; however, its uniqueness is not all positive. Given what the market expects from an American IPA (something hoppy and clean), this brew could use some cleaning up. We did enjoy the malt-to-hop balance though.

The beer received a rating of 68/100, or "poor." While some of the off flavors described in the review of the bottled IPA could partly be blamed on the disconnect between the beer's original design and the product created at the contract brewer, the biggest culprit was perhaps expectation—the market demands more from an American IPA, the review suggested. Specifically, the market expects more hops.

However, the review also points out the beer's biggest strength—the malt-to-hop balance. Not only do the hops play nicely with the sweet malt (like many IPAs it incorporates caramel malt, which adds color and sweet flavor, but it also includes Munich malt, which contributes to the body of the beer), but Andris tweaks the fermentation process slightly to encourage the production of diacetyl—a buttery tasting compound often considered to be an off flavor. The mix of the malt, the diacetyl, and the subdued hops gives Blue Hills IPA an uncommon balance not found on the shelves of most beer stores. Andris wouldn't have it any other way.

"I didn't want to brew another hop bomb," Andris said. "Everybody and their cousin brews big, hoppy IPAs. It's possible I could brew a better hop bomb than everyone else, but it's also possible that my beer would just blend in with all the other options.

"I'd rather make a beer that stands out compared to the other beers on the shelf. If some guy drinking beer in front of his computer turns his nose up and says, 'This doesn't have enough hops! This doesn't taste like an IPA should,' that means I'm doing it right."

Blue Hills IPA is an East Coast IPA in a West Coast world. In the early days of the current beer revolution, beer brewed on the East Coast tended to more closely resemble beer brewed in the Old World. Sam Adams, the East Coast's craft brewing giant, made its name by mimicking German styles and adhering to the fundamental principals of German brewing. Out west, where American hops are grown, breweries like Sierra Nevada were redefining classic English styles by infusing them with more and more hops. Sierra Nevada Pale Ale laid the framework for a new style, or at least a new interpretation of beer dubbed American pale

ale. Soon, breweries up and down the West Coast from San Diego to Seattle would begin a hops arms race that gave birth to the intensely hoppy version of IPA that dominates today's markets. The trend spread east, making the distinction between West Coast and East Coast IPAs essentially nil, but the moniker stuck.

Perhaps the best and most famous examples of West Coast IPAs are a pair of beers from Russian River Brewing Company in California's wine country. The Santa Rosa brewpub and brewery makes a double IPA called Pliny the Elder that is often ranked as the best double IPA in the world. Russian River brewmaster Vinnie Cilurzo's Blind Pig IPA is also a highly rated beer. The hops burst out of both of them, and there is a sort of citrus and floral paradise in the nose of each. However, the real beauty of these beers lies in the way those hops play with the malt. The flavors make a honey-flavored harmony in the drinker's mouth, and the beers are rightly celebrated for their excellence.

"In both cases the malt recipe, although simple, is very important when making these hoppy beers," Vinnie said. "For Pliny the Elder, it helps that the beer is 8% ABV, so there is a good amount of base malt in the beer. For Blind Pig IPA, since it is lower in alcohol, we also use some Maris Otter malt during the mash. This more expensive malt gives a good amount of body to the beer while still leaving a clean flavor. Simply put, having a nice malt foundation is very important.

"Another thing we do that keeps the beer clean-tasting is the use of sugar as a fermentable in Pliny the Elder. By doing this we get a very dry beer, which leaves a nice balanced finish. With this though we have to be careful to not add too much sugar, as it can leave the beer overly thin."

The shift toward West Coast IPAs coincided with a growth in popularity of beer from small brewers. It could be argued that the tilt toward more hop-forward beers was a major reason for the market expansion of small breweries. Unfortunately, it also brought along with it a vocal group of beer geeks who craved those hop bombs and gleefully bashed any beer that didn't live up to their standards. In Santa Barbara, brewmaster Kevin Pratt refers to this vocal minority as "the hopperazzi."

"They're constantly following the next hop sighting," he said. "Those are the people that are really driving the extreme edges of craft brewing. Unfortunately, they're also the ones trying to define it, and I find that to be—" He stops for a moment. "We were listening to punk rock when you came in: the Ramones and the Clash. I find that really great, guitar-oriented rock tends to be the music of the brewery because it helps you lift heavy things. [The hopperazzi] tend to be on the edge of those kind of fans that are of the belief that once [bands] become famous, they've sold out. You're not that good anymore if everybody knows who you are."

Kevin's sentiment is mirrored by Andris, who shrugs off negative reviews from online rating sites like BeerAdvocate. He doesn't hold disdain for the site, but he recognizes that its users aren't the market he is aiming for.

"The social media is just that . . . social," Andris said. "Any loudmouth can make anything up."

This isn't to say that brewers like Andris and Kevin don't appreciate the beer geeks who come in and chat them up about their methods and ingredients. But they also keep things in perspective. They recognize that it is impossible to please every segment of the beer culture, so they focus their attention on the things they can control. Mostly, that means making balanced beer.

Balance does not mean turning away from flavor. Although a beer geek that enjoys having her palate shredded by over-the-top IPAs might equate balanced with bland, beers like Pliny the Elder and Firestone Walker's Double Jack Double IPA are consistently ranked among the best beers in the world, let alone among the best double or imperial IPAs. The hops most certainly take center stage in both, but there is a structure to the malt backbone that supports the hoppiness.

"I'm a huge cheerleader for balance and drinkability," Matt Brynildson said. "I think you can have extreme, extreme flavors and still have balance. I use our Double Jack Imperial IPA as an example of that. There's a beer that's over the top in flavor and still has a drinkability factor. I think it's critical, but I think out-of-balance beer is fun too."

Matt continued to express enjoyment at sour beers that are growing in popularity and had a laugh at the way many beer drinkers now seek out beers so sour that they feel like they're tearing the enamel off their teeth. As Kevin pointed out, it is fun to sample beers like that, but that doesn't mean those kinds of extreme flavors should dictate what everyone drinks. And although those beers are fun to try, the more balanced versions tend to be the ones with staying power and the gravitational pull to draw the beer drinkers back into their orbit.

"When it comes back to the classic producers who have been making lambic and gueuze for decades, I think there's a balance to making great beer," Matt said. "That's just one brewer's opinion."

For many brewers, the concept of balance does not, and probably should not, stop with just the beer. A brewer who praises balance in the beer is likely going to preach harmony and moderation in other aspects of life as well. For Andris Veidis, this meant striking a happy medium between his home life and work life. Andris did his part at home to make sure that his son was taken care of when his wife went to work. In a similar way, he made sure his friends were happy by being the designated beer supplier for family gatherings and barbecues. He may not have been able to hang out with his old band as he did before he owned his own business, but as long as he made up for it by bringing kegs of Blue Hills beer to the gatherings, they got over it.

Like his IPA, Andris avoided tilting too far in any direction. His approach did not stem from a bland nature but from a level-headed pragmatism.

When the mash was resting, typically for about forty-five minutes or longer, there was little to do in the brewery—especially in the early days of Blue Hills, when there were fewer accounts to satisfy and therefore fewer bottles and kegs to fill. After the hops were measured out in the cold room and the cleaning solution was noisily pumping through the tank for which the day's brew was destined, Andris had time to chat. As in any workspace, the conversation covered every topic from work and business to relationships and politics. During the 2008 presidential campaign, Andris expressed his doubts about both candidates.

"I have a hard time getting behind McCain," he would say. "But then again, maybe I should vote Republican if Obama is going to raise my taxes."

He said the last bit with a playful tone to his

voice, but it was clearly a concern. Although there were no plans to directly increase taxes on breweries put forth by either candidate, Andris understood that the likelihood of a higher tax rate for his business was greater under a Democrat than it would be under a Republican—especially in a political climate where conservative groups like the Tea Party were gaining power behind contradictory slogans like "Freedom isn't free!" and "Taxed enough already!"

But it wasn't the hyperbole of fringe groups or the rhetoric of the politicians that had Andris concerned. As a small business owner, he recognized that businesses like Blue Hills already face significant tax costs. Not only are there the standard costs of operating, but there are fees for licenses that must be acquired at the federal, state, and local levels. Many states, Massachusetts among them, also require breweries to pay annual excise taxes. Finally, the federal government taxes each batch of beer.*

---

*In the United States, the final product is taxed. A standard practice for many brewers is to pump their beer from the fermentation vessels, through a filter, and into another vessel known as a bright tank (referring to the bright, or clear, beer inside). The amount of beer in that tank is measured and recorded for tax purposes and is then sent to kegs, bottles, or the taps in a brewpub. Although the task of recording the volume of beer falls on the brewer, this is not performed on the honor

For Andris, the decision was not as simple as one party versus another. The decision was weighed out in the same way, at least in spirit, as he balanced the bitterness of his beers with the grain bill when formulating a new recipe. Unfortunately, in politics, there is rarely the opportunity to find that harmonious point in the middle. Perhaps this is why conversations in the brewery may drift to politics from time to time, but often find their way back to beer.

It wasn't unusual for the topic of beer to focus on what was new in the industry. Since Andris spent the first years of his career as the CEO of Blue Hills without taking home a paycheck, his personal beer budget shrank to essentially zero. If he wasn't at an industry event or a festival, which were actually fairly frequent, he likely wasn't trying too many new beers.

"You drink any good beers this weekend?" was a typical question he might ask one of his interns when they showed up for work on a Tuesday. The

---

system. Federal tax agents are frequent visitors to most breweries. Historically, countries such as the United Kingdom taxed their brewers on the raw materials used. Therefore, processes, such as filtering, which would result in lost beer, were avoided in order to avoid paying taxes on unusable product. This form of taxation would be similar to the United States government changing its policies to tax income before things like health insurance were taken out.

beers that always drew the most attention were the ones from out of state. It wasn't because Massachusetts didn't have anything good to offer—quite the contrary—but those new beers simply had more appeal. It was the same attention paid to the new kid in class. There's a brief trial period where that new student has a shot either to impress or to be cast aside. Like the pretty girl with the good clothes, sweet personality, and good sense of humor, a brewery that introduces itself with a quality offering is quickly embraced. A deeper relationship with the brewery might expose some of its flaws, but those can be addressed on their own time. And, like the kid who showed up on the first day with messy hair, strange mannerisms, and a penchant for saying rude things under his breath, the brewery that leaves a bad first impression with uninteresting beer often isn't given a second chance.

Along these lines, breweries in today's market are beginning to rethink earlier strategies regarding expansion. When a beer gains a certain level of attention, either by winning awards at major festivals like the World Beer Cup or Great American Beer Festival or by building a significant amount of hype and attention on Web-based forums, distributors begin to take notice. When distributors take notice, they approach the brewery with offers to distribute its beer to new markets. As small breweries grow in popularity, many begin sending their beer anywhere that will take it. Sometimes the destination was at the behest of distributors, and sometimes it was driven from within the brewery.

On the surface, this system seems like a no-brainer. How could it be a bad thing for a brewery to expand its market footprint by working with an out-of-state distributor? Wider distribution means more sales, and more sales mean more money. Unfortunately, many breweries discover the hard way that unchecked expansion can cause unforeseen problems. The biggest problem is when demand outgrows supply. Again, it seems like a good problem to have, but if a brewery is unwilling to take on new debt in order to increase production, there is no way to adequately meet the demand of the market. This may not have a huge financial impact on the brewery, but it does not help the brand. This is especially true when breweries distribute out of state but struggle to provide the local market with enough beer to keep the shelves stocked.

The most notable brewery to encounter this problem was the Delaware-based Dogfish Head. In March 2011, Dogfish Head founder Sam Calagione published a blog entry titled "Thanks for Understanding" that detailed the reasons why they would no longer distribute their beer to Tennessee, Indiana, Wisconsin, and even nearby Rhode Island:

We recently learned that, over the last five years, demand for Dogfish Head brands has made us the fastest growing brewery in America. We are proud of this growth and the opportunity we've had to turn so many more people on to our off-centered ales. The most important thing for us (and we hope for you as well) is that we produced and sold a greater variety of super-high-quality, super-unique off-centered ales than any other year in our 16 year existence. In 2010, we did more R&D batches and more one-off-freak-flag-waving brews than ever on our 5-barrel system from our Rehoboth pub. On the production side, we brewed several new and different bottled and draft beers. Our success has also pushed our production capacity to the absolute limit.

We are sorry that some of you have experienced frustrations when you've recently asked for your favorite Dogfish beer at your favorite craft beer joint. While I've described our philosophy on balancing growth vs. the health of our company in a previous blog post, please know that I do recognize our choice to grow strong and smart instead of just growing fast, our choice to keep experimenting and pushing the envelope instead of allowing ourselves to be mutated into the 60 Minute brewing company, comes with its own challenges. We are up to the challenge and hope that you are too.

The move was met with what might best be described as unbridled fury by many of the customers in those states. Dogfish Head, as the blog entry points out, is one of the most popular breweries in the country. In Tennessee, beer drinkers were upset because the selection on shelves was already limited. Indiana and Wisconsin drinkers took this as another arrow in their sides, as other breweries announced similar pullouts from their states. In Rhode Island, there was general outrage that a nearby brewery would no longer make it into their local package stores. It was a sting made all the more confusing and personal by the fact that Dogfish Head would still distribute to Massachusetts. In all cases, many beer drinkers took the departure personally and vowed to no longer support the brewery—which, of course, they were no longer able to do anyway.

Dogfish Head wasn't the only brewery at the time to realize it had failed to meet demand, but it was just the most prominent one to do so. What Sam did not say in that blog entry was that the wide footprint made it difficult to ensure the quality of his products in those states. Whether that was a factor was unclear, but it is an element that many breweries must face when considering expansion.

When a distribution area is small, the brewer can ensure that his or her product is properly stored and handled. Vinnie of Russian River is notoriously picky about where his beers are sold. Although he brews some of the most sought-after beer in the country, the brewery remains relatively small and does not have a wide distribution. Chances are good that if Russian River beers are sold outside of Northern California or San Diego, where Stone Brewing Co. operates a well-regarded distributorship, they are sold because Vinnie already has an established relationship with the bar or store owner from his many years of experience in the beer community.

An understanding that Russian River beers will always be in demand comes with this approach, but it also demonstrates a dedication to the preservation of Vinnie's product and of his brand. If he were to be more lax and allow distribution to stores that could not guarantee shelf space in a refrigerator for his beer, then he could not guarantee that one of his customers might end up drinking a months-old Pliny the Elder that had spent the majority of its life sitting at room temperature. Although the online forum threads that pop up touting the drop-off of Pliny's freshness after just a few weeks are closer to hyperbole than truth, it is a known fact that double IPAs are best consumed fresh and that hop aromas fade over time. The only way to slow the steady degradation of beer, as with most food products, is to keep it refrigerated.

Although Vinnie is likely the highest profile figure in the brewing community to limit his distribution in order to maintain control, it is a common source of concern for brewers, who work with a sales staff that may be more inclined to find profit in a new market than to worry about the quality of the product. Sometimes, it is up to the brewer to intervene.

"I think it's the brewmaster's job that when the sales team says, 'Hey, let's ship some beer to Florida,' I say, 'No,'" Matt Brynildson said. "'Why?' 'Quality concerns.'

"I think we're really fortunate. I think from the very beginning we said we're not really interested in growing any faster than quality will allow us. Our growth pattern has been to just keep picking up states in the western region and going where the beer will be well received. We have a little bit of a seeding program, and that's where the East Coast sees our beers. We've picked good, developed beer markets. We've brought beer to market because we've been asked to, and not because we're trying to force-feed it. We put enough out there that the market demands and make sure that it's fresh."

● ● ●

Back at the hypothetical bar, the cast of characters and their faces tell a different story as the evening wears on. The friends of the Bud Light drinker arrived, and he moved with them to the table closest to the nearest television. A pitcher replaced the bottle, and he is pleased to share a round with his buddies. Something happens on the screen, and they all shout and raise their glasses before taking big drinks and ordering up another pitcher. The beer doesn't quite cool the fire from the wings they're eating, but it's good to have something to wash it down.

The woman with the Trappist ale finishes her final sip and calls the waiter over to ask for her check. She has had enough beer for the evening, and her boyfriend is picking her up to take her to that new French restaurant opening downtown. Near her, the hophead is midway through his second imperial IPA, and his glassy eyes peer off into the distance. When he finds his focus once again, he asks the bartender for the beer list, which she happily supplies. He takes another big sip as he's looking it over, seemingly not finding what he wants. The bar only had two imperial IPAs on tap, and he tried them both. He gives up and finally just asks, "Do you guys have any imperial stouts on? Preferably something barrel-aged."

The group in the corner, the one with the beer

drinker enjoying the well-balanced beer—their food just arrived. Hungry, they dive in. The food doesn't break up the conversations, though, and it doesn't slow the drinking. The slight smile that crossed the beer drinker's face after the first sip is steadily becoming a permanent fixture. When the waitress comes around to see if they need more beer, the table orders another round of the same. The beer drinker chats with the others with the glass in hand and points out that the beer is brewed at a nearby brewery. The group agrees that they should all go visit and take a tour next weekend.

★ 3 ★

"RAISING ALL THE BOATS"
BREWERS AS COLLABORATORS, NOT COMPETITORS

The three of them sat huddled over their smartphones, typing out messages and scrolling through e-mails. The constant hum and clatter of the bustling Stone Brewing Co. brewhouse filled the silence. Over the steady din, one of them spoke up: "I still like Alamo Fighting Water." The proclamation drew laughs from the others, who knew the name would be shot down by the feds, deeming it unseemly to put the word "water" in the name of a beer. They put their heads together a little longer but still could not come up with a name for their new beer. It would have to wait; it was time to add the molasses.

Mitch Steele, Stone's head brewer, was joined by fellow brewmasters Rich Norgrove, Jr., and Matt Cole. Each wore their own version of the brewer's uniform. Rich, the co-owner and brewmaster from Bear Republic Brewing Company, made the trip down to Stone's facility in the San Diego suburb of Escondido from Northern California. His salt-and-pepper goatee and rectangular glasses gave off a California-cool vibe that felt authentic. His Golden State pride was reflected in the brewery's emblem, essentially the state flag, which was emblazoned over his heart on his shirt. The right side had his nickname, Ricardo, printed in script.

Matt came in with Rich, wearing jeans and a long-sleeved shirt. During this period, Matt was busy upgrading his Ohio brewpub, Fat Head's, into a full-fledged production brewery. He exuded a different type of cool, with a red baseball cap and yellow-tinted shooting glasses resting on top of his head. He had a Gatsby-esque smile, a midwestern charm that made you feel more like an old friend than a virtual stranger.

Mitch, their host for the afternoon, was just as casual and approachable. Like Rich, he wore a button-up brewery work shirt. On the right side was a Fat Head's patch, a souvenir from a visit he had made to Matt's pub. On the left were the words "Arrogant Bastard"—Stone's aggressively hopped and high-alcohol American strong ale that has become, for many, symbolic of the American beer revolution. It rests perfectly in tune with the brewery's brash public persona, but fits Mitch not at all. He was shorter than the others, and his slightly tousled black hair, clean face, and understanding gaze gave him a fatherly aspect. His eyes shined with an intelligence that expressed itself in easy and elevated conversation. It was the kind of intellect necessary to manage the brewing operations of an ever-expanding brewery of Stone's size.

The three were in Southern California to brew beer together. This collaboration was to be a celebration of the pioneering days of the beer revolution, as the trio planned to brew a Texas brown ale. The style was all but lost among contemporary brewers, but it had been a staple of a previous generation, when it was embraced by home brewers and eventually developed into a mainstream product by Pete's Brewing Company in the 1980s.

"Basically it's an India brown ale. A lot of California brewers were the driving force behind it. It all stemmed from a home-brew shop in Texas that was selling kits to California brewers who were loading it up with Cascades," Matt said with an air of nostalgia. One could nearly picture him as a younger man, leaning over his kitchen stove pouring malt extract into a pot of boiling water, then dumping a small container of hops in, taking a moment to consider the effect, then dumping in a little more with an impish grin spreading across his face.

None of the breweries had anything to gain from the others' success; in fact, Stone and Bear Republic could easily be considered competitors. Both stand as representatives of aggressive West Coast beers well known for hop-forward profiles and a willingness to push the boundaries of their drinkers' palates. Ever since Sierra Nevada defined the style of American pale ale as a hop-first beer in 1980, breweries like Stone and Bear Republic have been defining West Coast beer as flavorful ales with high IBU ratings and bursts of hop aroma. Yet here they were, laughing at some of the sillier name suggestions, brewing together, and doing what they could to promote each other's brand. The brew was eventually named TBA—a hint at Texas brown ale but also at the difficulty in trying to come up with a name for it. It was delightfully hoppy in the nose, with bursts of citrus and grass overpowering every other smell. The first sip from a very cold glass tasted more like a highly hopped IPA than a brown ale. But, as it warmed, the malt characteristics were able to emerge and the punch of the hops became a nice complement to a smooth, almost chocolaty finish.

This collaborative brew day in the middle of December was the sixth of the year for Stone, but it is far from the only brewery to work this way. Brewers around the country (even the world, as the Sam Adams–Weinheinstephan collaboration for Infinium proved) have participated in collaborative projects with other brewers. Many times, the collaboration is between small breweries from entirely different markets. However, regional competitors are not shy about helping out a neighboring brewery when necessary.

The practice is confounding in some ways.

When your competition struggles, you stand to profit. Even an industry as good-natured as the beer industry has to understand that the purpose of a business is to make money—right? What good can be served by allowing the competition to gain strength alongside your own business?

Stone's CEO and cofounder Greg Koch has strong feelings on the subject. Beer geeks recognize Greg as one of the faces of the beer revolution in America. He stands out even among the handsome and charismatic Sam Calagione of Dogfish Head, the professorial and dapper Garrett Oliver of Brooklyn Brewery, and the fatherly and friendly billionaire Jim Koch (no relation) of Boston Beer. Among the various personalities of this new generation of American brewers, Greg comes off as the most bombastic and brash (even if it's more of a public persona than an actual personality trait). Of the bunch, he is the only one who jumps on bar tops with a megaphone to launch a tirade against the evils of "fizzy yellow beer." He poses for pictures with fans while making his signature "Greg face," his mouth wide open, seemingly shrieking in rage. The Greg face is one element of a successful branding campaign that has made Stone Brewing Co. the (open-mouthed, screaming) face of a generation railing against unimaginative beer. In one-on-one conversation, Greg exhibits a far more demure nature. The arrogant bastard shouting through a megaphone transforms into a humble, self-deprecating beer nerd who seems to be happy just to be included in the discussion. It's easy to forget that he is the CEO and public face of one of the largest and most successful breweries in the United States.

And for a successful brewer, collaboration isn't without some advantages. Putting the livelihood of others, even your competitors, over profits can make for good PR. Many small brewers consider the big guys like Anheuser-Busch InBev to be the real enemy. Helping other small brewers can lead to a more competitive marketplace that, in turn, helps them all. Still, there had to be something more concrete than just solidarity and goodwill to justify this type of sleeping with the enemy.

"I don't know if we really think about it from that perspective," Greg said. "I don't have a ready answer. What do we have to gain? I don't know. It's fun. It's cool, and we like it."

Seriously? It's fun? A multimillion-dollar company that, in many ways, sets the standard for doing business in an industry decides to collaborate with its competition because it's fun?

"It's something cool to do. I suppose I could really extrapolate a lot and say, 'Well, we like to promote camaraderie in the craft brewing industry. We love showing the craft brewing industry doesn't need to, and usually doesn't, behave like the commodity industry; that things like collaborations can be for reasons other than strategic.' Definitely not everything in craft brewing needs to be strategic. Maybe most of craft brewing isn't strategic.

"Strategic is thinking out from a business perspective and key coefficients and matrixes and that stuff. Maybe I don't think about it from those perspectives because I'm not capable of doing it from that perspective. I have to read Dilbert comics to understand it, and even after that I don't really know what's going on."

Greg was being humble. It takes more than an elementary understanding of business strategy to achieve his degree of success. But to him and brewers like him, financial success isn't the only thing. If it were, Stone likely would have avoided overloading its beers with hops—the most expensive ingredient in beer in terms of price per pound—and focused on cutting costs rather than expanding palates and pushing boundaries. Industrial brewers aside, American breweries are focusing on making a quality product first and profits second. It is an appealing notion that seems to have been lost among the skyscrapers of Wall Street, where the emphasis is on quarterly earnings reports, shareholders, and dividends.

With beer, we don't have to understand those things. All that matters is what the beer tastes like. It was comforting to hear that Greg shared a similar view. Strategic or otherwise, Stone was not in the habit of making bad business decisions.

Since its inception, the brewery has been expanding—both in terms of production and market share, as Stone is now listed as the eleventh largest craft brewery and eighteenth largest brewery overall, with nearly 180,000 barrels produced in 2012 and steady growth since Greg and cofounder Steve Wagner began production in 1996, with four hundred barrels produced in about five months. Even if Greg, Steve, and the business team in Escondido made most of their decisions based on what seemed like a cool thing to do, their instincts were clearly pointing them in the right direction. When beer bloggers and fans on Twitter started buzzing about another Stone collaboration in early 2012, I decided to visit to learn a bit more.

I arrived at the brewery at about eight a.m. Mitch was already there, of course, but he was still up in his office when I was greeted by Stone's public relations coordinator, Randy Clemens, an occasional contributing writer to *BeerAdvocate* and coauthor of *The Craft of Stone Brewing Co.: Liquid Lore, Epic Recipes, and Unabashed Arrogance*. Randy showed me around the grounds a little bit, including the impressive World Bistro and Gardens. The massive beer garden stands apart from the rest of its industrial corner of Escondido, in close proximity to what seemed like a dozen car dealerships. About the time we finished our tour, Mitch came down and introduced himself. Rich and Matt were still on their way in, but there were already complications.

"Looks like we'll have to do a little problem solving when they get here," he said to Randy. Randy had suggested to me that there was some sort of mishap with the grain order, although he didn't know the specifics yet.

"What happened?" he asked.

"We ordered the toasted wheat malt, and we thought it was going to be flaked. It's not flaked. We can't throw this in the mash without milling, and it's too late to add it to the mill." In order for the sugars inside the malt to be accessible, the grains have to be crushed in a mill first. A flaked grain, like some types of oat and a handful of other flaked wheat malts, isn't protected by a hard kernel and can be added straight to the mash. Some brewers order their grains precrushed, but many have their own mills. And while some breweries would be able to interrupt the process to mill the grain and add it to the mash, Stone's mostly automated system wouldn't allow for any interruption after the process had begun. When Rich and Matt arrived shortly after, Mitch pitched the problem to his collaborators. Rich eyed the bag of toasted wheat that Mitch had included as evidence and Matt inspected.

"It's your brewery, what do you think?" asked Matt, the most loquacious of the three.

"Well, we're going to be doing three batches, so I figured we could just increase the ratio of toasted wheat in the other batches to compensate," Mitch said. The others quickly agreed. As is the case in many breweries, the fermentation vessels held more beer than the brewhouse could produce in a single turn. Often, several batches were pumped into the same vessel. This allows breweries like Stone to save space with one large fermentation vessel rather than three smaller ones.

The next decision required a little more deliberation. "We never came to a solid decision: Do we want to add molasses or brown sugar? Or both?"

Matt was the first to respond. "I've never been a big fan of adding sugar to my beers."

"I add sugar to my brown ale," Rich added, just loudly enough to be heard over the din of the brewery that was beginning to come to life, with its forklifts and workers buzzing around tending to the everyday tasks of a busy brewery. Matt conceded.

"In that case, maybe we should do it. What do you think, Mitch?"

"We brought in some molasses in case we want to do it, so I say we go for it."

"Okay." It hadn't taken much to persuade Matt that adding the adjuncts was the right thing to do. Clearly, there was respect for one another's knowledge and talents in this arena. And it wasn't as though the adjuncts were being added to shave costs or dumb down the beer in order to appeal to a wider audience. Still, he had his questions. "Will this change our plans at all? Is this going to move our projected gravity?"

Mitch answered this time: "Yeah, it's definitely going to raise our original gravity up a point or two. It shouldn't be too much, though, we can figure it out pretty easily, I'm sure." They could. The brewing team at Stone was capable of determining how such changes would affect the brew with some simple calculations.

Rich added, "Mostly what it's going to do is add some more unfermentables that are going to add to the complexity and flavor." These sounded like good changes.

With these points settled, the brewers headed off to check on the mash. Unlike smaller breweries, where a brewer might add grain by hand or at least mix the mash with a handheld rake, Stone's process was automated and highly mechanized. A conveyor belt carried the crushed grains into the mash tun through a covered pipe where it was sprayed with water to reduce dust and then combined with hot water to convert the starches to sugar.

"Do you guys spray your grain to keep the dust down?" Rich asked.

"We do, but it's still a major problem. We vent it out the roof, and we have to keep cleaning the solar panels up there because they get covered in dust and don't work as well."

The conversation centered on the practicalities of the brewing business. Neither Bear Republic nor the production brewery Matt was building for Fat Head's handled the scale of production that Stone did; both men seemed eager to pick Mitch's brain to see what he thought of the equipment.

Mitch should know. Prior to Stone he was an assistant brewmaster for Anheuser-Busch. He had worked on bigger systems, but he started his career on smaller systems in some of the earliest brewpubs in the United States.

Mitch led our group on a tour of the brewery, while Rich took out his cell phone and snapped a picture of some metal box with switches on its face and a bunch of pipes coming out the top heading in several directions. He sent it to one of his employees, saying, "He's going to flip out when he sees this." The equipment turned out to be a system for pumping caustic chemicals and phosphoric acid throughout the brewery to clean the tanks, a task that might be relegated to an intern or volunteer at a smaller brewery. The brewing procession continued to geek out as Mitch led it through a small section set aside for aging beers in whisky and wine barrels. (Stone also boasts a much larger facility specifically for barrel aging, with this smaller section at the brewery reserved for beers in the early stages of the process that could be checked on easily by the brewers.) By now, everyone was caught up. There was very little to do but wait for the first bit of wort, called the first runnings, to be extracted from the mash tun and sent to the kettle.

With a moment of downtime, Mitch explained why Stone was so fond of collaborating with other breweries.

"I think the general goal is for us to do about four a year," he said. "One a quarter, and that fits in with our release schedules and special releases and stuff like that. We like doing them because they're fun and they generate some excitement. From a brewing standpoint, not talking about the business, what's fun about it is doing things that we wouldn't normally do. Doing an old-school hoppy brown ale like we're doing today, that's not something that we would have on our books to do. It's kind of a cool way to get creative and have some fun and do interesting things."

But were there any added benefits to collaborating with skilled brewers like Rich and Matt?

"Absolutely. Always. It's like everybody comes in with some different ideas on what a beer should be and what you should use in it and, yeah, you always learn something. Even if it's just the experience of brewing a certain type of beer."

That exchange of knowledge was reflected earlier in their discussion of molasses. Neither Matt nor Mitch was very familiar with it as an ingredient in brewing, but Rich knew through his experience that it could be used to add complexity to a brown ale. Likewise, Stone Brewing Co. had reportedly never made a beer using Cascades hops before, at least none that Mitch could recall, but both Rich and Matt had made West Coast IPAs using the citrusy hop many times (it could be argued that Bear Republic was built on Cascades, since many of the brewery's IPAs are bursting with the grapefruit aroma characteristic of the hop). When it came to adding Cascades, both during the boil and to the fermentation tanks to dry-hop the beer, Mitch was able to rely on his collaborators' experience.

The spirit of collaboration runs counter to what you see among the big brewers. Budweiser and Miller spend a fortune attempting to cut the competition out of the minds of their customers. Yet here were a group of small brewers working together rather than fighting for every beer drinker. Why were they so adamant about helping one another out?

"I think the big part of it is the small brewers, when they started out, they had a common enemy, and that was the big brewers," Mitch said. "Big brewers are so business oriented and so concerned with each other that they've gotten in the mode of not sharing anything with anybody. The way we look at it, if we're helping somebody out or somebody has a question or we have a question and we want to ask somebody, it's all about the rising tide raising all the boats. That's what's going on, and we feel very strongly about that. That's one of the things that I think is cool about our company is we sell thirty-five different brands of craft beer through our distributor. It's all about increasing. We all want each other to do well because it helps everybody if we're all doing well. . . . There's still a lot of room, and there's room for everybody. At this point, we don't look at other breweries as competition, whereas the big breweries look at everybody as competition. We look at it as more kind of a collective effort to change the beer-drinking habits in the country."

This was the attitude in areas of the country where small brewers flourished—such as San Diego. Brewers like Stone Brewing Co. began to grow to the point that their iconic black tap handles were more common than the Bud Light shield in local bars. (This is not to say Stone is a giant. It is still incredibly small compared to Anheuser-Busch InBev and even pales in comparison to breweries like Boston Beer Company, New Belgium Brewing Company, and Sierra Nevada Brewing Company. Where Stone produces close to two hundred thousand barrels of beer per year, Boston Beer makes closer to two million. Neither is close to giants like Anheuser-Busch, which brews hundreds of millions of barrels of beer annually.) Suddenly, the small brewers aren't so small. But Mitch says they've stuck to their small brewing spirit.

"I think we've held pretty true to that all along," he said. "I haven't seen any changes in that aspect. I think as we've grown we've had to implement things internally that make it more challenging to keep the small brewery mentality and feel to things. Just as a natural progression you have to implement policies and procedures and things like that that some people perceive as us getting too big, but in general this is why we do things like collaborations. My only day when we're brewing to be out here in the brewhouse all day is when we're doing a collaboration. Otherwise I'm pushing papers on a desk and answering e-mails. It's just a way for us to keep it fun, keep it creative and crafty, and all that stuff."

While competition among members of the industry exists, it's often friendly. Breweries strive to best each other at competitions like the Great American Beer Festival and the World Beer Cup, but the focus of those events is more on the camaraderie between beer makers and beer drinkers. The medals make for a nice display back at the brewery, but ultimately the GABF and WBC are better known for their beer-tasting events and after-parties. Instead of striving for market share, brewers are generally satisfied to share their turf. Granted, there have been several well-documented lawsuits and legal spats between breweries over names and labels. (For example, in 2010 Port Brewing, which makes and sells the Lost Abbey brand, brought a suit against Moylan's Brewing, in which Port took objection to Moylan's use of a Celtic cross similar to the Lost Abbey trademark. Tomme Arthur, cofounder of Port Brewing, and Port took a lot of flak in the online beer forums and blogs for the move, probably because it resembled similar actions brought against brewers from companies outside of the industry, such as a cease and desist order from George Lucas sent to New England Brewing Company demanding that they stop producing their popular Imperial Stout Trooper—they didn't, but they did change the label from a straight-forward storm trooper's mask to one sporting a classic Groucho Marx nose-and-mustache disguise.) But for the most part it has been a harmonious existence.

Like Rich Norgrove showing his fellow brewers how to utilize adjuncts in a beer, collaborators are able to lean on the strengths of their partners to complement their own skills. This is not to say that breweries invented collaboration or that they have somehow perfected it. They have, however, embraced it. Breweries like Stone Brewing Co. and Boston Beer Company are showing that the bigger players can get in the collaborative spirit as well.

So, would Miller and Budweiser ever come together to make a true Bohemian pilsner? And could this collaborative model be transferred to other industries? What would happen if Toyota collaborated with Chevy to create a full-size truck that operated on a hybrid engine? That these partnerships are so hard to fathom is part of what makes the idea feel so special when it's found in craft brewing.

The brewers themselves go about it without a second thought. During a lull in the process, Matt, Rich, and Mitch took a break for lunch. They chatted about the industry—but mostly they just chatted. They sampled the More Brown than Black IPA, a collaboration between Stone, The Alchemist, and Ninkasi that had been released that day. It felt like three guys hanging out together on a Sunday. There was no discussion of what anybody's role was in the collaboration or how they would split the profits. There was no suggestion that what they were doing was even anything very special. It was just three guys getting together and making beer, the same thing that happens in kitchens and garages all over the country.

It just seemed like a fun thing to do. They might be onto something.

★ 4 ★

"EVERYBODY IN LANCASTER HATES EACH OTHER"

A FRATERNITY OF BREWERS

On the day the hop shipment didn't arrive, there was enough snow at Blue Hills Brewery that the massive piles formed by the snowplow took up several spaces in the parking lot. It was another cold morning in southeastern Massachusetts, and the whole region had just been rocked by a snowstorm. I kept on my coat and carried my rubber boots into the brewery. It wouldn't be much warmer inside, but soon I would be hefting fifty-pound bags of grain into steaming-hot water, so I wouldn't stay cold for long. Andris was already busy. I spotted him on a ladder checking the water temperature in the big blue hot water tank used to feed brewing water into the mash tun. Steam spilled out and gave him the appearance of a mad scientist working on his latest diabolical creation. I shouted good morning, put my boots on, and prepared to work.

"Oh good, you're here early," he said. "We've got a bit of a problem, and we might not be brewing today."

Sometimes I got the feeling that he purposefully

left details out of stories just to see if the other person was interested enough to ask a follow-up question. I took the bait.

"Why wouldn't we brew today?"

"Because we don't have enough hops."

That was a good reason. We were supposed to brew a batch of Blue Hills India Pale Ale. Beer geeks scoff when I cite this beer as one of my favorites because it doesn't have the typical overpowering hop presence of other American IPAs. In most, hop aroma is the star of the show. It dazzles the drinker with a bouquet of citrus and pine, and the first sip smacks them in the mouth with bitterness and hop flavor. The sweet malt flavors come in second and help encourage another drink with a crisp finish. In Andris's IPA, the hops played a subtle role, serving as well-balanced complements to the overall flavor of the beer. It was closer to an English-style IPA, and used U.S. Goldings hops—an American-grown strain similar to the U.K.'s East Kent Goldings.

"We are all out of the Goldings," Andris explained. "We were supposed to get a delivery of them this morning, but the shipment got delayed because of the blizzard."

"Oh. So, what do we do?" It was cold and early. No beer needed to be filtered or kegged, and most of the kegs were clean. If Andris decided to call it a day and blame it on the snow, I wouldn't mind heading home for a few extra hours of sleep before getting ready again for my evening job at the paper.

"Let's plan to brew anyway. Set up eight more bags of two-row, and I need two more bags of crystal malt." He pointed to the platform near the opening of the mash tun where he had already stacked about ten bags of grain. "I'm going to make some phone calls."

As I lugged bags of grain onto the platform, Andris dug out a somewhat mangled-looking book. It was a directory of brewers in the area, and as he spoke loudly over the ever-present hum of the cooling units and the various other noises in the brewery, I could hear his side of the conversations.

"Hey, this is Andris at Blue Hills, how are you guys doing this morning?"

A pause.

"Good, good. Listen, we had a problem with our hop delivery because of the weather, and I was wondering if you had any Goldings that you could spare.

"Ah, you were expecting a shipment of them too, huh?

"Alright, I'll give them a call. Thanks, and let me know if there's anything I can do to help you guys out."

I wasn't sure who he was on the phone with, but after he hung up, he looked at me and said, "I think I may have found a solution. They didn't have any, but he told me that Mayflower always has a ton of hops on hand and they use Goldings. I'm going to give them a call; if they've got some, then I'm going to go down and buy them off them. While I do that, you can start the brew."

Those last words stuck to me. That would be my first time brewing alone, so it took a moment for me to realize the significance of what Andris was doing. Mayflower was arguably one of Blue Hills' biggest competitors. Although there were plenty of beer bars with dozens of taps in Boston, the rest of the region was typically made up of sports bars, restaurants, and dives with only a small handful of taps. They carried Bud Light or Miller—something to pour by the pitcher when Patriots fans crowded in on Sundays. They carried Sam Adams Boston Lager or the area's most successful regional brew, Harpoon IPA—maybe both. Typically, these bars and restaurants also had a seasonal from one of those breweries and then a fourth tap (Guinness Draught was popular as well, but it is served on a nitrogen dispensing system that is typically separate from the standard tap towers). This fourth tap was reserved for a small, local brewery. If a bar decided to carry Mayflower on draft, it most likely would not have room for Blue Hills.

Tap accounts were the lifeblood of the business—especially in Massachusetts, where breweries are not allowed to sell beer from a tasting room. So what was Mayflower doing lending Andris a hand? It would have been easy to say, "Sorry, man, we can't help you out today—we've only got enough for our own schedule."

Mayflower was only about forty miles away from Blue Hills, but with the snowy weather I knew Andris would be gone for a while. While he was out, I imagined the tense interaction between him and Ryan Gwozdz, the head brewer at Mayflower.

"Good day, Ryan."

"Andris."

In my mind the two stood face-to-face, staring at the other's eyes, waiting for the other to blink.

"They tell me you've got Goldings."

"Maybe I do, maybe I don't."

"Look, man, I'm not trying to get something for free. I'll pay you."

"Damn right you'll pay. One hundred dollars per pound."

In the imagined showdown, Gwozdz had a competitor begging for product. He could demand any price he wanted, even if it was far above market price. If Andris wanted to brew, he would have no choice but to give in. I dumped more grain into the mash, pacing myself so that it had time to mix enough with the incoming hot water and the powdery grains didn't bunch together in dough balls. When I had started as an intern at the brewery, I was too slow at the process and the mash was a little too watery by the time I had loaded all the grain. Now, I was practiced enough that I had to exercise a modicum of patience while pouring.

Once the grains were in, there was nothing to do with the mash except let it sit for forty-five minutes while the enzymes converted the starch to sugars, which the yeast would eventually turn into alcohol. As I waited, I sanitized the fermentation vessel into which we would later pump the finished wort. As the pump sent the solution through the clean-in-place system, I wondered again what must have been happening at Mayflower. What if Mayflower refused to sell Andris hops? What if they could not negotiate a fair price? Would all this wort be wasted?

It was time to run the vorlauf, a process of recirculating the runoff from the mash back over the top of the mash, to clarify the extract by running it through the grain bed, which acted as a natural filter to remove excess proteins. When some grains were sucked into the runoff tubes and slowed the process, I flushed them out by hooking a hose up to the system, just as I saw Andris do before.

He had been gone for nearly two hours as I started sending the mash extract into the kettle while simultaneously adding more hot water into the mash tun. This process, known as lautering, served two purposes: first, the hot water denatured the enzymes in the mash and put an end to the starch conversion process; second, the hot water rinsed the grains clean, ensuring that as much sugar as possible made it into the kettle. The extract would be boiling in another hour or so, and if Andris didn't return with some hops the whole process would have been pointless. I started to imagine some solutions in case he came up shorthanded, but struggled to think of anything short of drastically altering the recipe.

Fortunately, my worries were unfounded. Andris walked in moments later.

"We've got hops!" he shouted, a Cheshire grin on his face. He didn't look like he had just endured the grueling negotiation I imagined. He was carrying a box of hops, as well as a grocery bag full of something else

"Did you have to pay a lot for them?"

"Nah. I told them I'd get them back later. It's all good." So much for the showdown.

"Sorry I took so long, we got caught up. How's the brew going?"

I told him the mash went well. I mentioned the plug up during the vorlauf, and my remedy.

"It works every time," he said, still grinning. Brewing suited Andris well, and he seemed glad to have the opportunity to keep going that day. "Check it out, they threw in some extras for me."

He produced a few vacuum-sealed foil packages. I recognized them as hop pouches. Inside were different forms of varietals, kinds we didn't use at Blue Hills. The box was full of Goldings pellets, but the bags had whole-leaf Cascades.

I was surprised. I certainly didn't expect Mayflower to be so helpful as to throw in extra goodies. Weren't they supposed to be Andris's competitor?

"We're all in the same position," he said. "We're all part of the same community. You'll learn that about this business. Yeah, they're our competition, but they know that if they were in the same position as we are that we'd help them out. We used to do this sort of thing all the time when I worked at Boston Beer Works. We'd borrow or buy hops from Harpoon all the time. It's not a big deal."

And that was that. We brewed. When all the runoff was in the kettle, I pulled the hot grain out of the mash tun. We ate lunch, and as the wort was pumped into the fermentation vessel, I headed off to my newspaper job. I still had that satisfied feeling of being part of a community in my heart. It was like two men competing for the greenest lawn in the neighborhood but loaning garden equipment to each other when needed and talking fertilizer over a beer. It felt good, and natural. Then, at the newsroom, I heard grumblings coming from the advertising side of the facility. A local business had begun advertising with a competitor and didn't see a need to place an ad in our paper as well. The sales manager was heated, and was talking loudly with the editor in chief—demanding that we not cover the local business's upcoming event. Instantly, that sense of belonging to a community left me, and I missed the beer world.

Southeastern Massachusetts was my first beer community. Under the shadow of bigger breweries like Sam Adams, and even Harpoon, the local guys were allowed a sort of freedom to play around and do as they liked. Beer festivals were an opportunity for them to meet, exchange brews, and get a sense of what their neighbors were getting up to. Together, they were like a cross between a band of misfits and a nest of gossiping birds. Brewers took breaks from pouring beer at their booths and gravitated toward their colleagues (no such thing as a competitor at these festivals).

"Did you try the new beer from Pretty Things?"

"What's with that guy's mustache? What's his deal?"

"Yeah, I know. But did you try the beer?"

"Yeah. Pretty damn good. How about that stout from John Harvard's?"

And so on.

At larger festivals, like the American Craft Beer Fest in Boston, brewers took the break between general sessions to circulate the room and hit up breweries from other regions. Often, they traveled in packs with the brewers they knew from their own area. Brewers from the Pacific Northwest came to see what the guys from San Diego were doing. They came to compare notes and see who was doing the most with their hops. East Coast brewers huddled together and discussed the nuances of open fermentation at places like Maine's Allagash Brewing Company, and Midwest brewers showed off their impressive array of bourbon barrel-aged imperial stouts. After years of restrictive laws that stymied creativity were slowly lifted, southern brewers seemed happy just to be a part of the larger community.

These cliques of brewers were representatives of the same regions that draw so much attention from beer drinkers. Any beer geek worth his or her tasting goblet could tell you about the best spots to hit in Oregon. If they hadn't been, they were planning a trip to the Great American Beer Festival in Denver and knew all the nearby breweries worth a visit. They might have grown up in New England and would speak fondly of the summers they spent winding their way through Massachusetts, Vermont, New Hampshire, and Maine—making frequent stops at every tiny brewery they found. They might point to North Carolina and the new brewing facilities in planning for Sierra Nevada, Oskar Blues, and New Belgium alongside myriad small brewers and claim that therein lies the future of the beer industry. These strong communities are places where brewers communicate, and more often than not work in collaboration rather than competition.

To experience a strong beer community, you might head to Bend, Oregon. Although it is a small town, Bend is consistently at or near the top of the list in terms of breweries per capita. Places like Boneyard Beer, 10 Barrel Brewing Company, and Bend Brewing among many others make it a beer lover's haven. So many in the area either grew up drinking beer made by the biggest brewery in town, Deschutes, or spent time working there as a brewer.

Jimmy Seifrit left Deschutes to take over as head brewer at 10 Barrel, where he oversees production on two systems: a fifty-barrel brewhouse to maintain the kind of production levels necessary to turn a profit and a ten-barrel system used to experiment with new recipes. He described the atmosphere at 10 Barrel as something akin to a playground.

"It's got a lot of personality, and when you have a lot of personality you create this aura where everyone is super excited because everyone is feeding off each other's energy. We try to keep things loose as possible." Jimmy was only describing his own brewery, but he may as well have been discussing Bend as a whole.

For another glimpse into what it means to be a

part of the beer community, a beer drinker could grab a meal at The Brew Kettle just outside of Cleveland, Ohio. The little brewpub is inconspicuous and unpromising, just another storefront in a dreadfully plain strip mall, but inside awaits something special. Underneath a comically mounted white tail deer (the butt end, not the rack) is a chalkboard loaded with a very serious beer list. Scattered among a bevy of some of the best beers available in the region lie a handful of beers brewed on premise, with only a TBK written next to them to set them apart. There is no hesitation in putting their beers alongside some of the best in the United States, and for good reason.

I visited the brewpub/beer bar one afternoon with my twin brother, Steve. It had been a long day of driving, and I was ready to hand the keys to Steve, so I went for the double IPA brewed by the TBK team. This style was insanely popular at the time, as the high alcohol and heavy amounts of hops made it easy to hide flaws in the brewing process, and the intense flavor was attractive to a brave new wave of beer drinkers revolting against light lagers. There are plenty of mediocre double IPAs on the market, but this was not one of them. The hops greeted me warmly in the nose, as did a hint of alcohol. The toffee-like sweetness and bitter hops played together nicely on the palate and covered enough of the high-alcohol burn that warmed the throat on the way down. Steve's

Witbier was equally impressive and not over-poweringly floral, as this kind of wheat beer can sometimes be. If visitors were in the mood to join even further into the beer community, The Brew Kettle offers them the opportunity to brew their own beer on a series of six half-barrel kettles in the back of the brewery.

In that innocuous strip mall space, TBK was a microcosm of the beer community in general. With its own beer standing side by side with the greats—some categorically better than anything brewed on-site—TBK appeared to welcome its role in that community. The same was true in Austin, Texas, at Black Star Co-op Pub and Brewery, where brewer Jeff Young puts his beers in the same tap lineup as several guest beers—often world-class guest beers. He holds no pretense about the importance of fitting in to the community as best as possible.

"We have tasting panels when our beers are done, and we get feedback from our tasters. Probably the most important thing about all of it is what's selling," Jeff said. "What are we making money on? Because ideals or no ideals, what really matters is the money about it. If we're selling way more commercial beer than house beer, then that's bad. The margin is much bigger on house beer and this is our place, so we should be selling better house beers.

"We have an awesome lineup of commercial

beers. Three-quarters of it is some of the best in Austin and Texas, and then the other quarter is some of the best from around the nation. That's tough for me when I see that; I'm like, 'Shit, I've got to compete with that? That's not even fair.' It makes me have to step it up. Sometimes I do, and sometimes I have to be honest and say I have to do better than this if I'm going to be competing with (Stone's) Sublimely Self-Righteous or something like that."

If you wanted to find a less-popular beer community, one where all the collaboration and friendly competition still inspired brewers to constantly check their own progress and products against their neighbors, but without the familiar faces of Bend or the all-in-one approach of places like The Brew Kettle and Black Star, you would do well to visit the breweries around Lancaster, Pennsylvania. Matt Keasey introduced me to the region, as he showed me around several locations before ending at his own: Spring House Brewing Company. The breweries in the area formed clubs for regulars, known as mug clubs, in which the patron would have his or her own special mug at each taproom and often some sort of discount that went along with it.

"Everyone kind of gets along," Matt said. "The people who are mug club members here are mug club members at other breweries around town. If I release something special, they'll take my stuff up to the brewer at the other breweries and vice versa. The people around town talk about the other breweries. It's not like a competition, and the patrons don't view it as a competition. To go around and visit all the beers the city has to offer is pretty cool."

That was the idea. Matt was to lead something of a brewery crawl in an effort to visit all the breweries in the region. It began in nearby Adamstown, the home of Stoudt's Brewing Company—the region's oldest and largest producer. Matt arrived along with his head brewer, Chris Rommel, and headed inside. It was in the dead of winter, and the weather was fittingly very cold. Matt, the heavier and older of the two, was dressed in jean shorts and a short-sleeved button-up shirt. His arms and legs were slightly pink where they came in contact with the cold air, but he didn't seem to mind. He gave the impression that he wasn't going to let a silly thing like the weather dictate how he should dress. Chris, who appeared younger than his twenty-odd years, was more covered up with jeans and a jacket. It was about noon, and Stoudt's didn't open to the public until four, but Matt put in a call to head brewer Brett Kintzer, who let the group in and gave something of an unofficial tour. Brett had a blue-collar appeal and sported a long-sleeved shirt and knit cap. He simultaneously appeared to be hot and cold—a result of working around steaming kettles one minute and in a cold room the next. What was planned as a brief tour and tasting turned into nearly three hours of Pennsylvania beer history.

Brett explained the history of Stoudt's (it includes a brewery, restaurants, antiques, festivals, and a car collection); he discussed the popularity of the beer and the current brewing facility's ongoing expansions. He poured a flight of beers, and it was noted how the brewery had mastered lager production over the years in its Gold Lager, a multimedal winner at the GABF and World Beer Cup, until finally the brewery crawl resumed and the group headed down the road toward Union Barrel Works.

Reamstown and Tom Rupp's Union Barrel Works lie between Adamstown and Lancaster. Unlike New England, where the brewing tradition comes from the British Isles, Pennsylvania boasts a strong German population. As such, it is deeply entrenched lager territory. A brewery like Stoudt's might make fine American pale ale, but it will always be known for its lager—at least in Pennsylvania. Union barrels, on the other hand, are the British system for fermenting ales (the kind featured in the two photos adorning Matt Brynildson's wall at Firestone Walker). Union Barrel Works, however, had nothing to do with the kind of English ales associated with the method—or with the English brewing method in general.

Tom was once the head brewer at Stoudt's, and the man lives and breathes lager. His dopplebock was rich and smooth. It was a lager well-suited for drinking in the cold weather of the winter months. Tom, who is middle-aged and wore a mustache and glasses, was working behind the bar, and the four of us chatted over pints and steak sandwiches.

The conversation started with why Tom preferred to brew lagers but quickly shifted into a carping session about the other area breweries and brewers. It was like getting a firsthand look at a family's inner squabbles.

"We're thinking about heading over to Saint Boniface from here, what do you think about those guys, Tom?" Matt asked. Tom kind of shrugged. His weathered face did not mask his look of disapproval.

"Those are those guys with the little nano brewery, right? They make all those imperial stouts and triple IPAs and things like that?" Tom didn't give his opinion on nearby Saint Boniface Craft Brewing Company, but he didn't have to. His expression said it all. There was no reason to expect a lager lover like Tom to get on board with the experimental and radical ale brewers down the road.

"Yeah, that's them." Matt said this with a sneaky grin on his face. He was agitating Tom on purpose, but he moved on. "Then we were going to head on into Lancaster to see Bill"—meaning master brewer Bill Moore at Lancaster Brewing Company.

"Those guys know what they're doing. Sounds like a good trip," Tom said.

We finished our beers and sandwiches, paid Tom, and headed on our way to the small town of Ephrata, just outside of Lancaster.

On our way in to Saint Boniface, I joked with Matt, "So these are the guys brewing all them fancy imperial stouts, eh?"

Matt chuckled a little. "Yeah, these are the new kids on the block."

"Tom didn't seem to think there was anything too impressive about them. What do you think?"

An impish grin came over his face when I asked him that question. It was the same look he had when he was prodding at Tom earlier.

"I think Sean is starting to figure out that I lied to him earlier when I said we've got a great beer community here"—this was addressed to Chris—"when, really, everybody in Lancaster hates each other."

Chris and I laughed. If he hated Jonathon Northup, it wasn't very obvious. Jonathon founded Saint Boniface in 2011 along with Mike Price. Mike wasn't in at the moment, but Jonathon was there to give a tour of the tiny operation. In one corner stood the small brewing system that produced only a few barrels of wort at a time.

Along another wall ran a shelf full of specialty ingredients. Plastic fermentation vessels kept cool by an air-conditioning unit filled an adjoining room. Jon, a tall man who appeared to be in his late twenties, perhaps early thirties, dominated the room. His bald head and bearded face gave him the appearance of a tough guy, but his friendly nature betrayed him. He and Matt greeted each other warmly, as Matt introduced me.

"This is Sean, I'm taking him around the breweries in the area so he can see how much we all hate each other."

"Watch out for the guys at Spring House," Jon said. "They're the worst of everybody."

Matt beamed at the insult and explained to him the situation.

"We got stuck at Stoudt's and spent way too much time there, so we're not going to dick around. Why don't you go ahead and pour us some beer."

Expectations regarding the imperial stout being poured were tempered by Tom's disapproval, as well as a lack of a reliable temperature-control system on the tanks. I fully expected to drink a mess of a beer that was either overloaded with dark malts or bursting with off flavors from an uncontrolled fermentation. What came out instead was a fine stout. Hints of fruit complemented the dark chocolate flavors, and it finished surprisingly easy. After the big and boozy stout, it was time for small tastings of Saint Boniface's Brutus Strong

Ale and a wheat IPA. The wheat IPA stood out the most, as the bready and sweet wheat malt complemented the beer's aggressive hop character. The flavors were intense, bordering on extreme, and the beers would be difficult to enjoy several nights a week, but both made for interesting experiences—which is the whole point of a nano brewery. Both Mike and Jon had other jobs, and Saint Boniface was mainly a project of love. By renting a small place and brewing small batches, the brewery's overhead costs were relatively low, and operating at a high profit wasn't the main concern.

"The beauty of this small system and the taproom here is that we are able to experiment a lot," Jon said. "We have a few regular beers, and we are working on getting those beers on tap at restaurants and breweries here in the area, but here at the taproom we are able to play around and try new things. If it doesn't turn out great, or if it isn't very popular, then we only have a few kegs of it and we won't have to worry about it taking up a ton of space forever. If it's great, then we can always brew more."

Matt was finishing a pint of the Brutus Strong Ale and kept his running joke alive. "This beer is shit," he said after gulping down the last drops. "Let me try that wheat IPA."

As Jon poured, Matt noticed a large plastic jug on the shelf of specialty ingredients labeled Belgian Candi Sugar.

"Which beer did you put this shit into?"

"None of these beers here. I actually hate that stuff, do you want it?"

Chris chimed in, "I was actually thinking about using some of that for a batch on our pilot system, Matt. We could use it."

"Thanks, Jon, do you want anything for it?"

"Nah, man. You guys helped us out so much in the beginning, plus I'm never going to use that stuff again. Just take it."

On the way out, as Matt tossed the jug into the back of his truck, he explained what Jon meant. "When those guys were getting started, it seemed like they were always over at our place bumming yeast and hops off of us."

The whole situation was reminiscent of Andris borrowing from his neighbors. Instead of a cup of sugar, Matt was leaving Saint Boniface with a jug full of it.

It was already dark outside when the brewery crawl found its way to Lancaster Brewing Company. It would be our last stop before Spring House, since it was starting to get late, and extra stops would result in bad driving decisions. The brewing company's two-story building's main floor was the top one, where patrons came to drink and buy merchandise. There was a rail and then about twelve feet of space from the edge of the floor to the wall, between which rose rows of tall, narrow tanks that stretched from the first-floor brewing facility to the ceiling. It was a great setting to enjoy a beer, the taproom perfectly integrated into a working brewery.

Hop Hog IPA was the drink of choice at Lancaster Brewing Company. It's a fully loaded and highly hopped beer that was the praise of all the area beer geeks. The praise was well-deserved, and the insightful beer was clearly the work of a master. That master, Bill Moore, joined the group for a pint, as Matt once again explained that he was trying to prove how badly everyone got along in the local community of brewers. Bill didn't miss a beat. "It's true. Everybody in Lancaster hates each other."

Beards are like tree rings for a brewer, and Bill's gray-flecked and shaggy beard hung well below his neckline. The conversation ranged from the local breweries and earlier stops on the crawl to beer makers in Nebraska and the West Coast. Bill seemed to know about every brewery in every corner of the country. He and Matt got technical and discussed updates and upgrades in brewing equipment before we said our good-byes and headed off to Spring House.

The actual brewery for Spring House was located in a barn on Matt's property in nearby Conestoga. He used to operate a small taproom out of the barn as well, but the problems with that setup became evident quickly.

"My house was just getting swamped with cars

and people," he said. "I couldn't really control it. My property was getting to be too overwhelmed. The brewery has a typical driveway with an oversized parking area. It was getting so packed with people coming down for tastings, that's what made me decide to open up the brewpub a few miles away. The location wasn't set up for that many people coming in and out. It was getting pretty crazy."

Here at the taproom, Chris operated the small one-barrel brewing system on premise. This allowed the taproom to legally operate as a brewpub and sell food and allowed Matt to dodge through some of Pennsylvania's muddled alcohol laws. We were tired from a full day of drinking, but the taproom was just starting to liven up for the night. Chris poured a tasting flight, and all but one of the seven were enjoyable. At this point of the trip, my palate wasn't up to the task of detecting nuances and undertones. A beer was going to be either good or not.

The real spectacle at Spring House was the crowd that was starting to form. One patron had brought in his homemade version of a Randall tap, a device made popular by Dogfish Head that featured a tube full of hops through which the beer was pumped on its way from the keg to the spout. In theory, the extra contact with the hops added a boon to the beer's aroma. I never found a hop-filled Randall to have much effect, but a stout pumped through a coffee-bean- or chocolate-filled Randall was a beautiful thing. More came in and took their seats. Some were regulars and recog-nized the other familiar faces at the bar, while many were new visitors. These were the same customers that Matt had described earlier—the ones that made Lancaster feel like a great place for beer.

Ultimately, the community that was beginning to take shape at the Spring House taproom is the one that matters most. Without a community of beer drinkers who go from one mug club to the next, a brewing community couldn't exist. There is a relatively small portion of beer drinkers who take their passion for the brew a step further. Like wine enthusiasts before them, beer geeks seek out the finest and most exciting new options every chance they get. They read blogs about beer, and then they start their own blogs about beer. They plan road trips based around breweries they want to visit, and they jump on Internet forums to share their experiences with like-minded aficionados.

In general, it is a pleasant community to be a part of. Beer geeks congregate together at beer festivals, many times sharing bottles of their own home brew or something unique from their region of the country. They often drive the popular discourse about the new wave of American brewers, and they are at the forefront of consumer trends. But there is a dark side as well. Some beer geeks forget that they are not the only beer drinkers in the community. Their disdain for things that they deem unsuitable for their sophisticated tastes pushes them over the brink into the realm of beer snobbery.

Perhaps nobody understands this community of beer drinkers better than Todd and Jason Alström. The Alström brothers were aspiring brewers and founded *BeerAdvocate* magazine as an attempt to generate funds for the brewery they wanted to open. The brothers were at the forefront of computer technology as well and wisely created a Web site and a blog at BeerAdvocate.com that served as a place to share beer news and features. What that simple site and magazine became wasn't expected by anybody. The Alström brothers soon had a legion of beer geeks logging on to their site and subscribing to their magazine. The once-aspiring brewers morphed into the multimedia magnates of the beer industry, becoming sort of de facto ambassadors for beer geeks everywhere. In an e-mail, they explained the differences between a beer drinker, a beer geek, and the dreaded beer snob.

"A beer drinker is simply someone who enjoys drinking beer," they wrote. "A beer geek, who is also a beer drinker, is someone who is enthusiastic about beer. A beer snob, who is also a beer drinker and beer geek, is someone who thinks their palate and opinion is superior and looks down on others."

The majority of a brewery's customers fall into the first category—beer drinkers. They might not be the most knowledgeable, and they might not appreciate the experimental tricks and techniques a brewer used in making the latest batch, but they go out and purchase the beer and are the lifeblood of a successful brewery. The brewery that caters to the beer geeks, meanwhile, may end up with the best reviews and have the longest lines at beer festivals. But the most successful breweries will be sure to appeal to the casual drinkers too.

Beer festivals and pub crawls are some of the best places to meet and interact with beer geeks. Online conversation can be all too easily soured by misunderstandings (sarcasm taken the wrong way, for instance), but tagging along with a pack of beer geeks at a festival can be a wholly rewarding experience.

"It's always great to run into someone who's just as passionate as we are," the Alström brothers wrote. "Even after all of these years, we try to embrace every experience, as most beer geeks rule and none of us would be here today if it wasn't for them. To paraphrase Ron Burgundy, 'We've been coming to the same party for seventeen years now, and in *no way* is that depressing.'

"Most beer geeks tend to be the same [in person

as they are online]: those who are active and more constructive tend to be more social in person, versus the keyboard cowboys who are extremely reluctant to say anything if they can't hide behind an anonymous user name."

At the Spring House taproom, the dude with the homemade Randall was probably a beer geek. The crowd of beer drinkers at the bar to whom he was showing off his device had probably never seen or heard of such a thing but seemed excited by it nonetheless. The next day, one of them may have taken that idea and told it to another brewer at another brewery's taproom, and the Lancaster beer community would continue to share ideas and learn from one another— pretending to hate it all the while.

★ 5 ★

"SOMETHING TO BE PROUD OF"

BREWING FOR THE COMMUNITY

W e call this here 'black gold.'"

"What is it?" I asked.

"Worm castings."

My blank face spoke the question I felt too stupid to ask.

"That's worm poop," he said.

John Obert, Sr., and I stood in a muddy field over a black fifty-five-gallon drum. John's hands sifted through the deep ebony matter inside; his boots sunk ever so slightly deeper into the soft mud. My canvas Vans did the same. I was way out of my element.

We were tucked away a slight distance from the nearby highway that connected John's farm, J3 Organics, to Birmingham and the rest of Alabama—just far enough to feel like a rural setting, but not so far as to avoid completely the rush and roar of a busy road. John gave a tour of his farm just before sunset of a pleasant winter day. He pointed out the fresh topsoil where they would soon plant heirloom tomatoes that he said would grow well over six feet tall. Through more mud, he walked to a heaping mound of decomposing organic material. He poked around and dug a tiny crater in the compost pile, and I could feel the warmth as I held my hand near.

This trip to the farm was unusual. This was not a brewery, and although they grew food here, it was most assuredly not a restaurant. But still, this too was about beer.

At Good People Brewing Company, the questions of what to do with their brew after it is done are just as important as those asked before it begins. J3 Organics was the answer to one such question. Namely, What do we do with all this spent grain?

Every process involves waste. Apart from the gallons of water sent down the drain, the massive amount of sopping wet grain is the biggest waste concern for brewers. After soaking for nearly an hour in hot water, it leaves the mash tun significantly heavier than when it enters. Many home brewers just dump the steaming grains into the trash, or save a portion to add to homemade bread (or even dog biscuits). At the commercial level, many brewers seek out the nearest dairy farmer, since cows and other livestock love the still semisweet grain. But for most brewers there simply aren't enough cows nearby to eat up all the grain, and a good portion of it ends up in landfills.

For Jason Malone, Michael Sellers, and Eric

Schultenover, the founding partners at Good People, sending the grain to a landfill wasn't an option. Not only would the brewery incur the extra cost of having the trash company haul away thousands of pounds of grain per week, but it just seemed wasteful. So they sought an alternative.

First, they found Jones Valley Teaching Farm. The small farm and its greenhouses sit smack dab in the heart of Birmingham's inner city, and it used the grain in compost piles on-site. But that was a temporary solution, and as Good People's operations expanded, so too did its piles of spent grain. Until one day, at a beer festival, they ran into John Obert and John Jr., who were just getting started on something new themselves—an organic farm called J3 Organics (J3 for John and John Jr.).

"We had a worm farm at the time, before we turned into a large-scale composting operation, and they asked if the worms would eat the grain," John Jr. said. "At the time, they were putting out about one fifty-five-gallon drum a week, maybe a little more. Two or three at the most.

"We started incorporating that to our feed for the worms, and the worms really liked it. Then their output grain started to increase, but so did our need for grain, so it was kind of fortunate how we grew together."

The worm castings made for an excellent organic fertilizer, and helped J3 grow as a business. Soon, the Oberts shifted the focus of their farm. They went from specializing in worms to a larger composting outfit that produced incredibly rich and organic topsoil for local farms. The Oberts received contracts to haul away manure from the Birmingham Zoo, then mixed that with sawdust used as bedding at a nearby horse stable. But perhaps the most important component of the compost is the thousands of pounds of spent grain from Good People and a handful of smaller breweries beginning to pop up in the area. Nitrogen, a key component of a successful compost pile, is extracted from the grain during the mash in the form of protein. Active enzymes help release it from the grain, and the vorlauf process that brewers use ensures that most of that protein remains in the mash tun and does not go into the brew kettle—leaving all that nitrogen-rich goodness behind for the hungry microbes inside the compost pile.

"I'm not really sure what it is about the grain that works so well. It may be the carbon content and the nitrogen content," John Jr. said. "It's a great mix, but it's really microbially active too. You're producing the sugars. We get some of that. It doesn't all drain off in the mash. We get a really microbial-rich raw material. I guess the word I was really looking for was catalyst. It's a huge catalyst to create the heat, and it's alive when we get it. We mix it all up instantly when we get it back to the farm. Manure is also great because it can sustain the ability to provide organic bacterial growth and moisture content with things."

Better compost means more nutrient-rich top-soil, which means better crops. As I walked over the small farmland at J3 with John Sr., he pointed out where they would soon plant another crop of heirloom tomatoes and recounted a story about showing a family friend around the field when the fruit was in season.

"When they are at their tallest, they can grow well above your head," he said, lifting his arm as high as it could go. "We had to add extensions on top of the wire frames to give the vines something to support themselves. And they are good too. I was showing someone around here one time and he said, 'These look so good, I can't wait to take this home and eat it.' I plucked one off a vine and said, 'Why wait?' I took a big bite right here. It's all organic. We don't use any pesticides or anything, but he seemed shocked that you could just pluck one right off the vine and eat it. He was so used to buying his tomatoes from the store and taking them home and washing them before he ate them that he didn't think you could do that."

When they're in season, the tomatoes are sold to local vendors and restaurants interested in providing their customers with fresh food grown nearby. Jones Valley Teaching Farm, which uses topsoil from J3 Organics, also provides fresh vegetables to local restaurants and pubs like The J. Clyde, located on the same street as Good People's original facility. In this way, the brewing process goes full circle. Grain goes to J3, which sends soil enriched by the composting process to farms like Jones Valley, which sells vegetables to restaurants like The J. Clyde, which also happens to sell Good People beer.

"They do their thing with it [at J3] and combine it with other organic material and break it down to make organic planting supplements," Jason said. "It goes back to Jones Valley, who uses it to grow fruits and veggies, then back to the retailers, who sell our beer as well. What we do ends up at the bar across the street in the form of beer, but also the waste product in the beer-making process makes its way to the restaurant in the form of veggies that benefit a few people along the way."

The obvious appeal of a brewery to any local community is based on its primary function. Just as the guy with the kegerator and big-screen television is the assumed host for every big game, so too is the community brewery the go-to outfitter for neighborhood cookouts. But with Good People, simply providing their neighbors with beer isn't enough. Giving away their grain to J3 was a no-brainer because it solved a major logistics problem for the brewery, but their community involvement goes way beyond donating brewing byproducts. Jason and his partners frequently give away beer and open up their brewery's tasting room to host charity events.

"We're sponsoring as many events as we can," Jason said. "The community around us is very giving with charitable events from different organizations. Even not-for-profits need revenues to do the things that they do. Events around food or beer or silent auctions, we're pretty quick to donate beer to that, which they sell to help generate revenues to do what they need to do. We do that as much as possible."

Part of that means doing whatever they can to help local organizations such as the Black Warrior Riverkeeper, a group dedicated to the preservation and cleaning of Birmingham's Black Warrior River. Their dedication to helping the local community in any way is not just a form of philanthropic marketing; it stems from a desire to do real good.

"This is what they actually believe," John Jr. said. "They have events for the Riverkeeper and the people who take care of the watershed in our community because they believe in keeping the water as pure as possible to brew good beer. They're very aware of Birmingham and that this community has had an identity crisis since the steel mills were gone."

That awareness was evident in Jason's face when asked why he bothers with charity in the first place. He took a deep breath, his face seemingly weighed down by his long, scraggly brown beard, then returned with vigor.

"Because it's Birmingham, and there are a lot of things about this city that are fucked up. But things are changing, and things are getting better, and we feel like we should do what we can to be a part of that."

Jason is a humble and private man. He isn't prone to sharing his feelings without good reason, so he didn't elaborate much beyond that. But Birmingham residents know exactly how he felt when he spoke about his city.

John Jr. expressed his love for his hometown while placing it in proper historical context. There exists an understanding that the city's history involves hard truths, but that its present and future are moving forward.

"The only major event that Birmingham has had since the steel mills were gone has been the civil rights movement," John Jr. said. "So we had a huge identity crisis in Birmingham trying to figure out who the hell we are. All we have is this negative stigma of bombing churches, the KKK, and burning crosses. It's not something we think about every day in our businesses, but it is something we've all talked about when we finally sit around at the end of a six-month period. We're all very conscious and aware that Birmingham needs something to be proud of, and the food and wine and beer industry is something to be proud of."

Perhaps the best title that a Birmingham resident can bestow upon someone is that they are "good people." The saying works so well because it leaves room for human flaws—something the city of Birmingham is all too familiar with. It is a delightfully southern expression that gives credit to people trying to do the right thing, and it just seemed to be the perfect fit for Jason and his partners.

Jason explained that like any business, it was time to come up with a brand name. Unfortunately, it was more difficult than anticipated. "Our meetings kept on revolving around the fact that we wanted to conduct our business in a responsible manner, be socially responsible, be active in the community, and give back in as many ways as possible, and we were trying to come up with something that would reflect that," Jason said. "One of my buddies went to a party with his wife the night that we had all gotten together, and he was hanging out with somebody and a guy used the phrase.

"Any other time, it just would have gone right past him in the normal flow of conversation, but since it was on his brain it really resonated at the time. We just thought it was a really good representation of what we were trying to do and the folks we were serving. It's less about us and more about our customers and community. The folks who support us and the retailers out here."

Good People's community involvement is admirable. But there is so much more to being a positive force in the community than attaching your name to a few fundraisers here and throwing money at a charity there. A big part of why Good People can be such a positive force in its community is because Jason's top priority has always been to put out a product of high quality that the people of Birmingham could be proud of—even when restrictive laws and critics made that seem impossible.

Alabama is not Massachusetts. It is important to consider the location of a brewery when we consider its importance to the community. Pilgrims never landed in Alabama because they were running out of beer on board and needed to establish a brewery. There was never a time when dozens of breweries operated in Birmingham. And while Massachusetts has its fair share of restrictive laws concerning alcohol, few states in the Union come close to matching Alabama and its regulation of the beer industry. Until recently, it was illegal to brew or sell beer above 6% alcohol by volume (ABV), and home brewing was also outlawed. Along with an organization called Free the Hops (a grassroots operation that deserves far more recognition for its efforts in modernizing Alabama's beer laws than this casual mention), Good People helped change that law and celebrated by brewing a double IPA that clocked in at 9.3% ABV.

Snake Handler Double IPA is a wonderful beer that starts with a heavy caramel sweetness that fits with the character of the style and is followed by a massive dose of citrusy and floral hop flavor. The beer is an assertion of their independence and provides Alabama beer drinkers with an opportunity to take pride in a local product.

"There's a lot of folks who said for a long time you couldn't make a big hoppy beer in the South because it's too hot and people didn't like it," Jason said. "I just think it's so cool to see all the folks around in the middle of July in the summer, and the first thing we run out of is the hoppiest beer we have. . . . It's so cool because so many people said there's just no way that will fly."

Good People has taken it upon itself, alongside advocates like Free the Hops, to educate the local population about everything beer can be when restrictive fetters are removed, but its founders have never forgotten that it is a Birmingham brewery. Many brewers pride themselves on brewing super-hoppy West Coast–style IPAs, or ultra-traditional German lagers. These brewers are rightfully proud of their dedication to a certain style, and many produce beers that shine within those styles. But ultimately, their dedication to and their ability to thrive within that niche work because their local market accepts that sort of variety. In Vermont, or Oregon, where local customers have a massive array of breweries to choose from, finding a niche and thriving within it is the only way to build a successful brewery. But in Birmingham, Jason understood that the only way to succeed would be to keep Birmingham in mind.

"We're very passionate about being what a local brewery should be," Jason said. "We're dedicated to taking care of our local market before looking at expansion. We try to involve our local market as much as possible. There's something to be said about living in a city with a brewery. Most decent-sized cities these days have a brewery, so it's not a novelty. It's an expectation. One of the benefits is being keyed in and having pride in ownership of what goes on at the local brewery. We're just trying to be keyed into that.

"If we didn't get feedback from our local market . . . then we might as well be located in California. If all they get out of us is going to the bar and saying, 'Oh cool, they're brewing the same four beers again just like last year and the year before,' then what's the point of being in town."

This desire to operate within and cater to the local community is not specific to Jason and Good People. This desire functions as a driving force for many of the small breweries that have popped up over the years as Americans have begun reclaiming their beer from the mass-producing factories that sent the same product to every corner of the country for decades.

Few places are as tapped into the wants and wishes of the local community as Black Star Co-op. Austin is a bustling city full of youthful rebellion against all sorts of things—be it fast food, pop music, faceless fashion, or mass-produced beer. The downtown area, which draws as many tourists as it does locals, is a melting pot of dive bars and nightclubs that serve a wide array of beer from big names across the country as well as the smattering of small breweries that keep popping up around Austin. To a visitor, this was the heart of the city. But Black Star was a little farther out of the way. About seven miles north of downtown in the Crestview neighborhood of Austin, just off Lamar Boulevard, Black Star Co-op caters to the local residents and not the transient crowds of tourists and hipsters.

"It's the exact opposite of 'out of the way' for the communities here," Black Star brewer Jeff Young said. "I think that's an important distinction. Six years ago when we started coming up with these ideas, we always wanted to be a neighborhood place. We wouldn't be a neighborhood place if we were out of the way, and if we were out of the way we wouldn't be a neighborhood place. I think we're fortunate that we got this place because it was very thirsty for a restaurant or bar to open here, because this area isn't the cool spot."

Located in an industrial park next to a train station, Black Star has an unassuming façade that makes it easy to miss if you aren't looking for it.

"It isn't the hippest spot in Austin, but what it is is on the rise. Austin in general, the coolest parts of Austin you can only look back and say, 'I remember back before it got all out of control.' If you start thinking about some of the really cool spots in Austin right now like South Lamar and South Congress, well they used to be shitty, crack-whore-infested sketchy places, but they were cool back then. Because they were cool, people started coming in like, 'Oh, now I'm on the edge of Austin.' Then all the money started coming in because the people came in, and it built up and pushed out all the crack whores. It's cool, but it's not cool the way it was formed.

"I used to live in South Congress and had my car broken into and all that, and being back there in that time was cool and we enjoyed it, but it isn't what it is now. Now I'm living up here and we have Black Star up here and there's a strip club just a few blocks down, there's a couple hotels that are at best halfway homes. There's these really cool endearing places that you wouldn't find unless you came here purposefully with someone that knew what was going on. The fact that there are huge neighborhoods around here filled with people like me—thirty years old, have a decent job have a wife and maybe a kid and a house—because there's such a big, actually three big neighborhoods surrounding us, we were able to capture a big portion of all of them. For them, we're certainly not out of the way."

Jeff defied easy categorization. His head was shaven completely smooth, except for a neatly trimmed beard on his lean face. He was thin and wore glasses. He looked like scores of other young men in Austin, but not like any brewer I had ever met. He took as much pride in his beer as he did in the cold room where kegs were hooked up to draft lines. In order to save space, Jeff designed a system similar to overcrowded library stacks or archives. The kegs sat on floor-to-ceiling shelves with wheels on the bottom. While changing all the kegs at once would be impossible, the movable shelves allowed access to every keg when needed while allowing Black Star to pack the space full of beer. It's a brilliant piece of innovation.

Eventually, you stop being surprised by Black Star. Everything about it, from its brewer to its keg room, was just a little different. Even its origins differ from that of a traditional brewpub. Black Star wasn't founded by a veteran brewer looking to finally have control of his own place, nor was it the brainchild of a restaurateur looking to get into the beer industry. Black Star began as a grand idea by Steve Yarak, who wanted to build a cooperative drinking hole, and a few others who thought that was a good idea. Jeff was a chemist and a brewer without a job, and some friends of his from brewing school mentioned that they heard word of a local meeting for some people who wanted to start the co-op.

"We showed up in some empty yard with about twenty people," Jeff said. "Basically there were a couple dedicated people and their friends just to show support. The guy that called the meeting, Steven [Yarak], said, 'Hey, I want to do a pub that's owned by its regulars, by the neighborhood it serves.' Another guy said, 'Hey, I'm Johnny [Livesay]. I work at the local grocery co-op, here's the structure that we need for a co-op.' I raised my hand and said, 'Hey, I'm Jeff. I need a job and I really would like to brew beer for your guys, but more importantly I think if we have our own product, rather than just a pub, I think it would be more intimate for a community. There's more of a tie of producing something.' So, it started from there."

And it started with no funds. The co-op was formed in 2006 with seventeen members ratifying the by-laws. The next step was to figure out what their approach to the business would be and how they would get approval from the Texas Alcohol Beverage Commission (TABC) to brew on-site.

"Over the next three years, we spent that time with zero dollars taking membership [dues] to raise a little money, but also in that time we had to figure out what the fuck we were doing, because it hadn't been done," Jeff said. "There was nothing we could look to to model ourselves out of. We could look to co-ops and look at how co-ops are made and formed and run. We could look at brewpubs and how they are formed and run, but the union of those two proved especially chal-lenging because you're working with TABC—our local alcoholic code. They had no idea what to do with us."

The group had very little business experience— as in none. However, they were all really bright and very committed to making this project work. While trying to find ways to raise money, they stumbled upon a loophole specific to co-ops that allowed member-owners to invest as much as they wanted into the company. As the number of member-owners grew, so too did Black Star's push for investment. Each member-owner still had just one share, but those who invested more were entitled to more dividends once the co-op started making money. Eventually, they raised the money they needed—$600,000 in total—they voted on a location, and they got to work constructing their brewpub.

Part of that construction involved building what Jeff called a "barninsula." Much like the keg shelves, this was an innovation unique to Black Star. The bar extends beyond the traditional stools-in-front-of-a-bartender front to a long, wide finger that juts out into the dining room with stools on both sides. The idea is that customers, many of whom live in the neighboring communities, can get to know one another over a pint of beer and fine food. It's all part of the community spirit at Black Star, which prides itself on being member-owned.

That sense of pride is evident in the employees; even as the bartender rings you up at the register it feels as though he is welcoming you into his establishment instead of just taking your order. The role of member-owners is special at Black Star, because it allows the customers to make the decisions at the brewpub. Although there is an elected board of directors to steer the collective, member-owners have their voices heard when Jeff needs to make a new beer. They hold occasional votes on what beers should be brewed and when.

All of the beer was good, but the one that stood out was a rare bottle that Jeff had been hoarding. It was called Epsilon and had been a limited-release when it came out. It was a Scotch ale, a strong beer known for heavy malt characteristics, that had been aged in Scotch whisky barrels. He cracked open the wax-coated bottle and poured it into two glasses. It was amber and looked thick, almost like hot honey, as it poured out. It smelled like butterscotch, and I wasn't sure what I was about to drink.

Butterscotch is a typical off flavor in beers with too much diacetyl, and I was worried that this beer was going to be funky. It wasn't. The buttery notes played with the sweet malt in a way that made it almost like a dessert. There were hints of vanilla and peat smoke from the oak that played with the gentle hop presence.

Jeff was humble in reply to the hearty praise heaped on the ale.

"I am really proud of this beer."

But when it was suggested that he release it regularly as a way to drum up business, he resisted. "There's a lot of great breweries that do that with a lot of great beers, but I don't want Black Star to be known as 'the Epsilon brewery.'"

Ultimately, Jeff's goal was to be a brewery that was both owned by and served a community. That was more important than prestige—than establishing a reputation among beer geeks. As they might say back in Birmingham, that's what makes him good people.

★ 6 ★

"THE RECIPE DOESN'T MEAN SHIT"
THE CRAFT OF BREWING

The first thing you notice about a great beer is the way it looks: Underneath a cap of foam rests the inviting liquid. It might be sparkling clear, with tiny bubbles catching the light as they run to the surface, or it could be appropriately hazy and begging you to investigate its secrets. Whether it is the color of golden straw, thick amber, or deep black, it looks just right. A strong sniff hits you in the face with hops, or perhaps sends subtle suggestions of chocolate and coffee. That first drink is followed by a satisfied sigh or sometimes a simple "yep," affirming some unknown question to which that first taste was the answer. With a great beer, it just feels right. It gives the sense that what you hold was once held by another human and that person intended you to enjoy it.

It was like that at Old Forge Brewing Company. The small Northeastern Pennsylvania town of Danville was quaint, neither kitschy nor corny—just quiet. Streetlights and business signs illuminated Mill Street along the way to the brewpub. It was inviting and reminiscent of small towns in old Hollywood movies.

Old Forge was essentially abandoned on a late night in the middle of the week, but the staff didn't hesitate to welcome in new customers. After crossing through the unremarkable threshold, visitors are struck by the immediate and inherent originality of Old Forge. The empty tables and chairs seemed to glow in a way that felt as if scores of customers had just left, but their energy decided to stay for another round. The bar was made of big, wide pieces of pine. It was more inviting than the glorified composite countertop bars at other pubs, and it complemented the rest of the furniture perfectly. (There was good reason for this: Local woodworker Keith Kocher crafted the tables, chairs, and bar for Old Forge.) Hand-thrown mugs hung from hooks on the walls. Members of the brewpub's mug club had their names and a brief quote fired on the sides of the large vessels. One of the bunch had a member's name and the words "Surprise Me!" inscribed on it. The bartender said that this particular customer would come in, sit at the bar, and ask for his mug. When asked what he wanted, his response was always the same: "Surprise me!"

The beer itself was remarkable. A pint of Old Forge's Overbite IPA sent an almost overwhelming flood of floral and herbal hops to the nose. There was some caramel and toasted bread at the leading edge of the first sip, but it gave way to bitter and grassy overtones from the hops that seemed to perk you up. The finish was dry and begged not to take another sip, but a big gulp. The Kölsch, a lighter German style of beer and something of a hybrid between a lager and an ale, was equally refreshing. It boasted an amber-colored body and crisp white head that lingered for a moment before dissipating into the glass. It smelled faintly of dank, herbal hops and caramel. It was light and easy to drink, but satisfying in a way that left you wondering why bigger brewers couldn't craft something similar to pump out to the masses. With its subtle nuances and flavors, it leaves standard American light lager in its dust.

As I sat at Old Forge for the first time, I hadn't yet met the brewer, but I felt like I was getting to know him. I could feel his craftsmanship in front of me. Likewise he had never met me, but I assumed that he had beer drinkers like me in mind when he brewed. There was an undeniable pride in that pint.

It was a short trip, but my visit to Old Forge left an impression. Everything about the pub seemed to scream out about what was right in the beer industry. Old Forge founder Damien Malfara didn't set out to build a shrine to local artisans and craftsmanship—it just sort of happened that way. His original plan was to source the pub's furniture and dishware from a restaurant supply factory, but it turned out it wasn't going to be much cheaper than commissioning a builder.

"I said, 'You've got to be kidding me, there's no way,'" Damien recalled. "I'm looking at booths and tables and all of this other stuff, not that it was crap, but it was mass produced. I don't know, it wasn't even like it was that cheap. . . . I started talking and asking questions from local people here—who did they know and who could do this stuff—I was really surprised at the response and the local people who wanted to do this stuff for a reasonable price . . . they could easily charge a lot more for this stuff, but they worked for us and were very reasonable with the prices."

And when you take in their pub, it makes a kind of sense. Jay-Z is fond of rapping that "real recognize real." Well in Damien's case, craft recognized craft. For woodworker Keith Kocher, this wasn't just an opportunity to sell some tables; it was a chance to leave a mark on the town's only brewery. The same was true for potter Mike Hart, whose mugs and plates filled the dining room. For artist J. Mark Irwin, the custom-designed tap handles were a chance to install his art in a functional gallery where the small, unique sculptures of twisted metal could be appreciated as more than mere objects for visual consumption. All of these individual elements came together because Damien was willing to let others apply their skills to his brewpub. When these craftsmen approached him with their ideas, Damien responded with enthusiasm. "I gave them the freedom to do it [like they wanted] because they're the experts."

Those were the elements, and that was the attitude, that led to a successful operation. And the same elements that made his brewpub a fantastic place to grab a pint helped fill it to capacity and spur expansion. Old Forge Brewing Company became more than a Danville brewpub. Damien still brewed beer on the small system tucked into the corner of the pub, but Old Forge had expanded into a larger production facility where Damien and his team were able to brew enough beer to finally meet the demand at the pub, and they had recently begun packaging his beer in cans for distribution.

Two years after my initial visit, Old Forge beer was introduced to the Philadelphia market. And for all his newfound success, Damien's focus always drifted back toward the craftsmanship. At a release party for the brewery sponsored by their distributor and held at Philadelphia's Standard Tap, Damien said that surrounding himself by handcrafted work forced him to challenge himself.

"I can't cheat. Even in the packaging brewery, the worst part of the brew day is mashing in and getting the spent grain out because it's all by hand. It's twenty-barrel batches, and that's a lot of grain. It's a workout doing it. It's kind of like, in the back of my head, 'You know, what if things go well, maybe I'll get a quote to see what it would cost to retrofit this thing to do it for you.' And every time I have that thought I'm glad the guys who are working for me are on board. Our brewer, his name is Justin, and our cellarman, his name is Jason—they're just like, 'You can't do that, man. It wouldn't be made by hand.'"

I remember pouring bags of premilled grain into the mash tun at Blue Hills. The first bag was easy enough. The twentieth less so. I remember pulling over a thousand pounds of steaming-hot spent grain out of the tun and dragging buckets of the stuff to the back door. I took pride in those moments, and it made the beer I drank afterward that much sweeter. Damien spoke of his pride in making beer by hand.

"It is real. It is not cliché. Sometimes you see it on labels, but the beer that we make is true. We make it in small batches, it is handcrafted. I'm not saying that our beer is perfect, and I'm not saying I'm happy with everything. I'm happy to the extent that we're making good beer, we're putting it out, and we're starting to grow—but the same thing I said before: Our beer still has room to improve.

"That's the other challenge, and to me that's the fun in it. I love being able to brew creative beers and try creative things in the pub. Over at the production brewery we're not doing that. We're brewing beers we've made over at the pub in bigger batches, with high consistency and quality—and that's a huge challenge. That's my learning curve. So far I think we're doing it pretty well, but I do know I want it to get better. There's a lot of good breweries in Pennsylvania that set the bar high. For me, my fallback beers if I'm going out to a place are one of those breweries because I know they're going to be good, they're always going to be good, and I can rely on that. I want people to think that way about Old Forge beers—that no matter what style it is, they know it's going to be good because it's Old Forge."

Consistency. That's the hallmark of the biggest and best brewers. Say what you will of the Bud Lights of the world, it must be said that they are reliable. The big boys pump out millions and millions of gallons of beer with remarkable uniformity and efficiency. Consistency was the reason why it was harder to be a commercial brewer than a home brewer. A brew day at Stone Brewing Co. involves a talented staff of brewers huddled around a computer screen ensuring that temperature and gravity readings were within desired levels. But wasn't there something to be said for things with their unique nuances?

"There is. I'm shooting for consistency all the way through, but you're not always going to have it," Damien said. "We took a couple of the batches, the canned product side-by-side [with the draft version] and didn't tell which one was which. I had over a group of people, not experts—just people. I poured for them and said, 'Which do you prefer? Can you taste a difference? Is it from the same batch? Is it different batches?' . . . One of the comments that one person made was, 'Yeah I do taste the difference. If asked to order another one I would get this one and not that one.' I said, 'Okay, does that mean I should dump that other batch now? What does that mean?' But the response from everyone else was different.

"Since they knew they were different after the fact they could say, 'Oh yeah, now I can taste it.' The people with more sensitive palates might pick up on it better, but I just hope that our customers—and our core customers—are the types of customers who will appreciate [the differences]—as long as it's not a negative; as long as it's not a flaw or an off flavor. Things like that are problems, but if it's just a slight difference, then I don't know how bad it is."

Damien spoke between sips of a round of Old Forge beers. I was drinking the Bourbon Barrel Quad. Despite a high alcohol percentage, it was smooth and easy to drink. It was velvety and viscous on the tongue, with fruity aromas up front and a hint of oak that punctuated the beer's sweetness. Beer like this is not born on a whim, but through careful planning and manipulation of recipes. Sometimes that means poring over numbers and calculations; other times it's going with your instincts and adding what feels right.

"It's a process. I'm trying to teach that to our brewer now. He's picking up on it pretty good. I guess for me, the way I start—this stout for instance," he said, gesturing at the beer in front of him. "Well there's so many different types of stouts, I don't know if any fit into this category. All I know is what I wanted to put into the stout. As a home brewer I had made a couple of different variations, and I went from there. I could care less what style it fits into, as long as when I drink it it's something I like and I can continue to drink. It's not always about the recipe either. The recipe could be fine, but let's just say you want it to be a little drier—it's not dry enough. Then you look at those things. Or even the yeast maybe, you might want to look at that. There's so many factors that aren't recipe based."

Beer making is following a recipe, but it's also a physical process. Which is more important?

"The physical part," Damien said without hesitating. If he was going to take pride and credit for making his beer by hand, then it seemed that he was glad to assert that it was his handiwork that made the beer as good as it could be. "It's all crucial. From the milling of the grain—that's important, you don't want to mess that up, you want to get that right—to the ratio of the malt to water when you mash it in. The temperature, the uniformity, how thick or how thin it is. This is just the mash. Everything is crucial. You want to minimize splashing and the air contact with it when you're lautering. You want to do that gently. You want to do it right, you want to get clear wort into your kettle—you don't want astringency. You don't want to undersparge and not be efficient, you don't want to oversparge [add too much hot water after the grains have been mashed] and have tannins extracted. There's so many factors, and you haven't even gotten to the boil yet. To me, the process is the most important part of making beer and the recipe is secondary.

"I could be wrong, don't quote me like an expert, I've only been brewing for a short while and I'm sure there's brewmasters out there who would say otherwise. But from my experience with what I do, the recipe doesn't mean shit. If you screw up on a crucial part of your process, that's what makes the beer undrinkable. That's what ruins your product. That's crappy beer.

"I didn't talk about being sanitary and making sure everything is clean," he added. "That's the most crucial. Every step of the way there's so many factors. It's not that I don't believe in recipes, but you can make a good beer with one malt and one hop that's real simple. It may not win any awards, and it might not knock any socks off, but people will enjoy it and they will be shocked to know that it's that simple. I know 100% if your processing is right and you're a good brewer and do it right, I'm convinced that's the way it can be."

Damien was right: The mastery of the process is what sets apart the great brewers from the rest. Many beers available in the taprooms of small breweries across the country are marred by overly fruity aromas and green apple flavors. They taste more like a decent home brew than a top-notch commercial beer. Yeast is a finicky creature that can create off flavors and aromas if the temperature gets even a few degrees too warm during fermentation. When those same brewers show off their fermentation vessels—with no means of temperature control other than an air-conditioning unit—the source of those minor flaws becomes clear. Similarly, there are plenty of imperial stouts that taste and feel something like chocolate syrup that could have benefited from an adjustment to the mash temperature to allow the enzymes to break the sugars in the malt into smaller pieces— leaving the beer drier and easier to drink. These beers weren't necessarily bad, but flawed. The diligent brewer learns from these mistakes and develops as a craftsman, but only if he or she recognizes that the problem lies in the process, not the recipe.

The same can be said about any craft. It takes time to hone the skill. Some of it can be learned through trial and error, but the wisdom of a teacher or mentor is indispensable. No matter how accomplished, the craftsman's pursuit of perfection is never done. It's a journey that continuously requires you to seek the development of your skills.

Of course, it's an overstatement to say that the recipe doesn't mean *anything*. It was early in my tenure at Blue Hills when I walked in one morning, rubber boots in hand, and was greeted by an uncharacteristically serious Andris. He was always busy doing something to prepare for the brew day when I came in, but on this day he appeared flustered.

"We're brewing the XPA today," he said, trailing off. The Xtra Pale Ale was Blue Hills' "conversion beer," targeting the Bud Light crowd with an easy-drinking, slightly sweet golden ale. It was dry with a faint, floral hop aroma and a crisp finish. The beer didn't last long in the lineup, as Massachusetts beer drinkers didn't need much convincing to drink a full-bodied ale or stout during the long winters, but at that early stage for Blue Hills it was still a major portion of the portfolio. Andris went on to tell me how many bags of grain I should grab and prepare to load into the mash. His attitude wasn't improving as he barked out his instructions.

"Grab two bags of wheat malt. I've been getting complaints that the XPA is flat and isn't keeping its head well." That explained it. Andris didn't mind too much when the casual beer drinker criticized his beers; he understood that everyone had different palates. However, if he received pointed feedback regarding a specific flaw it often sent him into problem-solver mode. Andris was doubling the amount of the protein-rich wheat malt in an effort to boost head retention, since the protein molecules string together along with hop oils and a handful of other elements to create the rich frothy foam at the top of the glass.

Andris spent a good portion of that summer, the nascent days of the brewery, trying to figure out ways to boost the head retention of the XPA. He checked the carbonation process in his bright tank, he sampled dozens of pints from the brewery's tap (the hardest part of the job), and frequently experimented with specialty grains to solve the problem. In this instance, adjusting the recipe was the only solution—and it was his dedication to his craft that led him frustratingly close to the brink of madness in his efforts to perfect the recipe and solve the problem. His confusion and frustration only mounted as the minor adjustments failed to make any discernable difference in the finished product.

The beer had been pouring fine off the kegs in the brewery, but Andris's partner in charge of sales was still reporting accounts complaining of flat beer with no head. What neither Andris nor I took into account at that point appears to have been his partner's over-excited reporting. There had indeed been a problem with carbonation with one of the early batches, but that was solved when the next batch went out with the proper levels of gas. There was still one account that said the beer was pouring flat, but the others were more than satisfied with the XPA. One bar complaining of flat beer likely means the problem was on their end, and not at Blue Hills.

"For a second there, I was starting to worry that I didn't know how to make beer anymore," Andris joked. We celebrated the revelation with a pint of IPA. We had both tasted enough XPA that summer.

A lot is made of the term "craft beer." The Brewers Association, which coined the term, defines a craft brewer as small, independent, and traditional.* There is no assurance of quality, only an assumption. The onus lies completely in the production of the beer, not in the final product. As beer drinkers begin to revolt against the larger brewers and their subsidiaries, a lot of good beer gets overlooked. Drinkers pick up mediocre "craft

_____

*"Small" is defined as fewer than six million barrels of brewed beer per year. "Independent" means that less than 25 percent of the company is owned by a business or party that is not a craft brewer. "Traditional" means that it brews an all-malt flagship or only uses adjuncts to enhance rather than lighten flavor.

beers" over world-class beers from brewers like Chicago-based Goose Island (which was founded independently but is now owned by brewing giant Anheuser-Busch InBev). It is the same blind devotion to branding that this new wave of drinkers detests in an older generation where men proudly declare themselves as "Bud men" or "Miller men." This is not meant as a knock on the Brewers Association, which by all accounts has done a lot for the advancement of beer. But clinging to an arbitrary distinction and elevating those beers over others are no less closed-minded attitudes than refusing to drink anything but "your" brand of beer. The distinction between what is "craft" and what is not seemed necessary when there were only a handful of pioneering brewers bucking the big boys in the early days of the American beer revolution, but with around 2,400 breweries currently operating in the United States it can now be assumed that when someone is discussing an individual brewer, he or she probably isn't one of the handful working for A-B InBev or MillerCoors.

The problem with adding the qualifier "craft" before a beer or a brewer is the implication of craftsmanship. While there are so many, like Damien and the others mentioned in this book, who aspire to be craftsmen, there are others who see beer as a growing retail market—not the product of a lifelong passion. There are others still who come into the industry with noble intentions and loads of enthusiasm but lack the skills and experience to make a quality product. There are plenty of self-taught brewers who took a home-brewing operation to the next level by opening up a tiny neighborhood brewpub, and there are plenty who spent years and thousands of dollars studying the art and science of brewing in a handful of schools across the globe. Ultimately, none of that matters. All that matters is what it tastes like. Small, independent, or traditional don't mean good any more than big, corporate-owned, or modern suggest inferior. A table with two wobbly legs is a bad table, no matter whether its creator was small, independent, or traditional.

But it's easy to tell what a lackluster table is. With a beer, it isn't always so obvious.

Enter Ray Daniels and the Cicerone Certification Program. Ray might be described as the beer geek's beer geek. Among many other things, he is a talented author (his *Designing Great Beers* is a staple for any serious brewer or home brewer), a senior faculty member at the Siebel Institute of Technology, where he received a diploma in brewing, and the director of the Cicerone program. Cicerone comes from the Roman or Latin word for "guide," and its graduates can be seen as something akin to wine sommeliers. A master Cicerone, of whom there are currently only seven, would likely be able to answer any question anyone would ever have about beer, while a certified beer server (the lowest ranking in the three-tier Cicerone program) would make a great addition to a brewpub where the servers are expected to understand what they are pouring.

If you want to know what can go wrong in the brewing process, he's the man to ask. Basically, the answer is a lot.

"Let's start with the water," he said. "You can have source water that has iron in it, and if you don't catch that and remove it you'll have metallic-flavored beer. That's not good. You can use the water straight from your municipal supplier without carbon filtering it, which will leave the chlorine in the water, which leads to the formation of chlorophenols in the beer, which is a burning plastic, burning electrical wires–type flavor. That's just two quick things related to water. Both are errors that would be really easy to make if you basically said, 'I'm going to make some beer,' and you started to do it."

The chemical makeup of the water in various regions is what led to the variation in most early beer styles (as certain water profiles lend themselves better to hoppy beers, dark beers, pale beers, etc.), but modern brewers are able to combat water issues with mineral additions or simple carbon filters. Ray described the importance of using fresh hops, instead of old ones that can smell and taste like cheese, and properly malted malt, before discussing the most common mistakes. "Fermentation is probably the biggest source of off flavors. Poorly conducted fermentation can result in unpleasant or unwanted flavors. Diacetyl is a classic problem."

Try this: Go to the closest small brewery near you and see if they'll give you a tour. Take a look at the fermentation vessels, and ask the brewer how he or she controls the temperature on them. If they point to the air-conditioning vent in the corner, chances are good that the lack of careful temperature monitoring during fermentation is going to encourage a bevy of off flavors to develop. Some brewers have artfully managed to mitigate this issue through careful monitoring of the room's temperatures, and some manage to use their limitations to their advantage by designing beers that suit this style of uncontrolled fermentation, but both of these cases are less common than a brewery full of beers riddled with off flavors.

This is not to give the impression that the majority of breweries are producing a shoddy product (that was a major problem during an earlier boom of microbreweries in the 1990s). In fact, the opposite is probably true. "Fortunately, brewers are usually fairly well educated these days. Brewers do overall a pretty darn good job of making good beer," Ray said. Part of that education comes from programs like the Cicerone program or a classroom setting at American schools like Siebel or a handful of others like the American Brewers Guild and the brewing program at the University of California, Davis. Still many more brewers are teaching themselves how to brew, and they're learning quickly.

"It is possible to get pretty darn smart about making beer without ever taking a class," Ray added. "If you're super passionate about what you're interested in and that happens to be beer, there's [a] tremendous amount of knowledge available in books and on the Internet these days. And there are groups of people that talk to each other, both over the Internet and in person. I went to Siebel in '95, and I had been home brewing for about five to five and a half years. I knew a hell of a lot about making beer. A lot of the questions that I was asked and a lot of the things I was learning in terms of the theory and the things that would produce these sorts of off flavors were things that I was refining rather than coming to for the first time. A lot that I learned was practical operational stuff rather than the theory. I already knew how to make beer that tasted good, what I was learning was how to do it on the larger scale."

These are the exact problems Damien is trying to avoid as he watches his brewery grow. So much of the brewery's reputation relies on how it handles the finer details of production because those details are reflected in the product when things are done improperly. "I actually have this fear that the more we grow and the more success we have, that some of those small details may get overlooked," Damien said. "I think that's the challenge. It was always me focusing on that, now as we grow there's more people working for us, and we delegate more tasks, and I really need to ensure that they have the same eyeballs—that they're going to look at things with the same attention to detail, and that is the challenge.

"I take it as, like, a challenge that I want to accept. You know what, there are a lot of places out there that haven't done that. There's other places out there that are successful, but when you go to them people say, 'Well, it's not the same as it was in the beginning. Or it's not the same as it was five years ago when so-and-so was always around.' I think there probably are some people saying that about my place right now, but I want to take that challenge and say I can't just drop everything and always be around. But what I can do is do my best to select the right individuals that are the right fit for us, so that moving forward people aren't always saying that about our place."

That is the craftsman's dilemma. It is different for an artist, who doesn't have to please a wide array of people to sell a piece; he or she only needs to impress one patron. The brewer, on the other hand, has to make a product that will be well received in the market. He or she has to appeal not only to the beer geeks who key in on off flavors and missteps but also the casual drinker who wants to sit back with a beer and watch the game.

Sometimes, it seems as though it would be simpler to be more like the artist and less like the artisan. Instead of striving to produce something that will be commercially viable, an artist-brewer could make the beer he or she wanted and defiantly tell the public, "Enjoy it. Or don't."

"What I like isn't always what the consumers like," Damien said. "I will say that almost all the beers that I make, I do like them, but it's more like at the pub when we do our one-off beers [that I make the things I really like]. Any of the barrel-aged beers or anything unique and different, I do feel like, yeah, it's art. This is what I made whether you like it or not. It is what it is. I also hope the customer trusts me that I wouldn't serve it if I didn't think it was servable."

Damien takes pride in his work. If he got tired one day and decided it was unnecessary to properly mix the mash by hand or monitor the mash temperature, his product would suffer. If he failed to make the sacrifices he did but continued to sling his beer to the public, then his reputation would suffer.

At the launch party at Standard Tap, he was

surrounded by his friends and family. How could he expect them to respect him and his work if he lost that commitment to quality? Damien's dedication to craftsmanship was about more than the beer—it was about self-pride.

As he said good-bye to his family that night, and as friends and fans came up to meet him and shake his hand, it seemed clear that he could have been just as impressive at another craft. If he had a passion for woodworking, he could have designed those tables and stools. Had he developed a passion for motors and engines, he would have been a master mechanic. When I think about the plates, the mugs, and the tables at Old Forge, I think I learned something about dedication and what it means to be a craftsman. Damien is not alone in the beer community in his commitment to his craft, and we can all be grateful for that.

★ 7 ★

"THE MOST IMPORTANT THING"
PROVIDING FOR FAMILY

There was no beating Andris to the brewery. If an intern arrived and he wasn't there, then he had gone out and was coming back. In the dark of winter, well before the sun rose to offer whatever meager warmth it could to Canton, Andris was at Blue Hills preparing the brewery for the day's work.

Brewers are no strangers to early shifts, or even overnight shifts, but Blue Hills was still young, and there was no need to cram in several brew sessions into a single day. In the first year of operating, Andris brewed mostly on Thursdays. A busy week meant brewing twice, with the other days spent filtering, kegging, bottling, or cleaning. A brew session rarely lasted much longer than six hours, a slow pace by most standards, so there was little practical reason for Andris to arrive so early. Of course, when it comes to family, practicality rarely has any bearing at all.

On brew days Andris had been up since sometime before five a.m. His morning rituals went unseen, as he was the only one awake, but it involved breakfast and coffee before heading toward Turnpike Street and continuing the short drive to the brewery. Inside, and still alone, the slowly waking brewmaster went through a checklist of items for the day. The first step was turning on the boiler. The boiler generated the steam that was pumped through the jacketed kettle and hot liquor tank (the large tank of water used to provide hot water, called "liquor," for the mash and sparge). After a cold night in the cavernous warehouse space, the water in the tank took a while to reach the proper temperature* and needed the early start for the morning's session. After checking over the inventory to make sure that there were sufficient ingredients for that day's brew, Andris was back in his black SUV headed for home.

At home, just waking up, was the reason Andris went to work so early. His wife, Alysa, was getting ready for work and minding their oldest son, Talis. With the brewery still too young to turn a profit, Andris and the Veidis family were living off his savings and Alysa's salary as a nurse practitioner. With the sun now up, Andris helped make sure Talis got his breakfast and took him to Alysa's parents nearby for daycare. If he had

---

*Andris had a simple way of determining if the water in the HLT was hot enough. If he opened the hatch at the top of the tank and steam billowed out and the hatch was sufficiently painful to touch, it was hot enough.

time, he would take his two dogs out to the park to play a quick game of fetch. Then, it was back to the brewery. More often than not, it was all accomplished before a single employee or intern made it in. A couple of years down the road, Andris and Alysa would repeat this routine with their second son, Maris, and daughter Sondeila. By the time an assistant brewer stumbled in around nine a.m., Andris was full of pep.

"What's the matter? You tired?"

And if an issue with Talis arose—if he was missing an essential item that his grandparents could not locate—Andris would leave the brew session in the hands of his assistant to sort things out. If something serious was amiss, or if Alysa's parents were otherwise unavailable, brew days would have to be moved. Andris's schedule, and therefore the brewery's schedule, revolved around his son.

The concessions Andris makes in order to maintain a happy and healthy life are hardly groundbreaking. He, and many brewers like him, was simply doing the same thing that American men and women have been doing since the modern era. Raising a family requires personal sacrifice. For Andris, that meant sacrificing hours of sleep and bending his work schedule to suit his family's needs.

As Andris and others can attest, it isn't easy. In

order to support his family, Jim Koch threw himself completely into his business. In the process, he built the largest craft brewery in the country, but he admits to having missed a significant portion of his kids' childhood along the way. While Andris's day started early so that he would be able to physically take care of Talis, Jim's day began early in order to financially support his family.

"Honestly, it's very difficult and maybe impossible to be passionately committed to being a brewer and having a fully balanced family life," Jim said. "At least, I have not been able to do it. I have four, wonderful, healthy, successful kids; I'm about to have my fourth grandchild. It's worked. But it did not work through a great, balanced life, honestly. I left at six in the morning on Monday to go to San Antonio for a beer event, I was working in the market yesterday, and today I got up early and went to our brewery here in Boston. So, I saw my kids for—I got home at eleven thirty at night when they were finishing their homework, and I drove my daughters to school, and that's the time I've spent with them this week.

"Not every day is like that and not every week is like that, but a lot of them are. The idea that you're able to achieve this harmonic balance—if you're passionate about your work and it's demanding work that you're really engaged in— it's a fallacy. You do the best you can and you try to make sure everything gets what it needs, but you're not going to get what you want. What you want is balance, but what you're lucky to get is everybody comes out okay." In his pursuit of beer making, Jim was not only considering a way to support his own family. He was also preserving his family lineage of brewmasters.

Perhaps the issues that Jim faces might be different had he taken a different approach. By now, Sam Adams feels like a brand that was destined to be big because Jim had big ambitions for it. But what if he had more modest aims of simply making good beer and living a good life? What if he had incorporated his family life into his business plans?

He might have found himself in a similar situation to Russian River's Vinnie Cilurzo. Although he is credited as the mastermind behind the beer, he is quick to admit that his wife and business partner, Natalie, means just as much, if not more, to the company.

"The truth is, Natalie is the backbone of Russian River Brewing Company," Vinnie said. "Somehow we have found a balance between personal and work life. At the brewery the workload is split like this: Natalie takes care of the brewpub and the business side of the brewery. I oversee the brewing and the distribution side of the business. Obviously there is a lot of crossover and we share all big decisions—things like big-picture items are shared. I think what makes things work so well is the trust we have between each other, we trust in each other's skills.

"No sacrifices need to be made. With a love for beer, a strong business, and an amazing staff, Natalie and I find it pretty easy to balance what we do. You are not working when you do what you love. Natalie and I wouldn't do it any other way, and we don't know what we'd be doing if we were not in the beer business."

Just like other entrepreneurs, young brewers have to confront the challenges that come with starting a business. Of course, few of them will reach the degree of success that Jim and his Boston Beer Company have. But everyone measures success in different ways. And while there may be many brewers out there striving to succeed, there are very few quite like Steve Gorrill.

Years ago, Steve was known as the mildly eccentric, slightly goofy brewer and owner at Sheepscot Valley Brewing Company. Andy Crouch, in his book *The Good Beer Guide to New England*, describes meeting Steve at an event in Bar Harbor, Maine, where Steve brought along his own sidekick—a duct-tape monkey on his shoulder. This, coupled with a stranger recognizing Steve as "Sheep-Scotty Too-Hotty," a wrestling persona adopted by the oyster-farmer-turned-brewer, even though he doesn't wrestle, made him stand out as an entertaining and all-around amusing fellow to be around. That was a good thing for his kids, because their father was around a lot.

Just a few weeks before his oldest child, Robert, was born, Steve opened Sheepscot in a barn on his property in Whitefield, Maine—just twenty-five yards from the house. Steve, like Andris, was no stranger to early mornings. When his daughter was twelve, he coached her soccer team. In order to be at the practice fields on time, he would be up and on his twenty-five-yard commute to work starting at three a.m.

"It's been great. He's been able to be involved in a lot more," Steve's wife and Sheepscot co-owner, Louisa, said. "It's [different] now, because the kids are teenagers. Our oldest son goes to a high school where he boards there four days a week, so he's not home anymore. And our daughter is now at a high school near where I work. For the kids, it allowed them to be home a lot and their dad to be involved. He coached Allie's soccer team. You know, it's kind of been really nice. They've been lucky that way. It's been good."

Sheepscot was founded in the late '90s, around the same time as a slightly more popular brewery in Portland—Allagash Brewing Company. Allagash founder Rob Tod and Steve were both experimenting with Belgian-style ales when the rest of the country was just starting to appreciate English-style beers like IPAs and stouts. The Portland market loved Rob's unique approach to beer, and Allagash grew into one of the more successful breweries in the Northeast. The Whitefield market, meanwhile, wasn't quite ready for the coriander, cloves, and bubble gum flavors of the Belgian-style beers Steve was brewing, and a decision had to be made. Steve could either stay on his original course and focus on getting his inventive beers into markets where they would be appreciated, or he could change what he was doing in order to suit the needs of his local community. Had he chosen to make Portland his target audience, there was a chance he could have sold a lot of beer and made a lot of money. However, it would have meant leaving Whitefield and little Lincoln County behind.

When Steve considered his options, he realized that there was only one choice he was willing to make. He abandoned the Belgian-style brews in favor of beers like his flagship, Pemaquid Ale—a malty, Scottish ale well-suited for the semirural area's cold winters but light enough to be enjoyed on the picturesque summer days as well. The decision was only made easier by Steve's desire to stay close to his family.

"I could actually sell quite a bit more beer if I wanted to get on and do that, but then I wouldn't spend more time at home, and I kind of need to do that," Steve said. "It's good to be around for your kids. [Family] is the most important thing."

Pemaquid Ale and Sheepscot in general came to be loved by Whitefield, and so too did Steve. He took on the nickname "The Count of Whitefield" and began inviting the town to the brewery in his barn every Thursday. Visitors might come for a tour, but mostly they came to drink. The event morphed into a community potluck. The town would come in, share some food, drink some beer, then go home. It was a comfortable routine that allowed Steve to do his job, support the community he loved, and stay close with his family. In many ways, it was a perfect fit.

Unfortunately, nothing so golden could stay.

On April 12, 2013, Steve Gorrill collapsed. Louisa received a call from a friend and came home to find him dazed and somewhat incoherent. Louisa, an occupational therapist, knew enough to have him sit down and rest while they checked him out. Steve was unsure of what had happened and wasn't able to communicate well enough at the time to articulate exactly what was going on. Louisa and her friend assumed that he had slipped and hit his head, that he was suffering from a concussion, and that he would need to see a doctor. The EMTs arrived and shared that assumption and took him to the hospital.

Once there, the doctors discerned that he had, in fact, endured a seizure. They guessed that the seizure had caused him to fall and hit his head and assumed that was the reason for his concussion symptoms. They decided to run some tests and to scan his brain to check for damage.

The situation went from bad to worse, as the scan showed a tumor in Steve's brain. Further tests would eventually reveal that it was stage 3 cancer and that Steve's life was in peril.

"We kind of went through a period where the news kept getting worse each step of the way," Louisa said. "That was kind of tough. Until recently, and now we've kind of had to accept that, yes, it's a tumor. It's always going to be there. It's going to come back, because that's what they do. It's cancerous, but now we've had some more positive things come out with the genetic testing that make it hopeful to respond better to treatment and be slower growing. I don't know. It's just a matter of taking things one step at a time. That's all you can do."

The tumor was in his brain, and surgeons were able to operate and remove nearly all of it. Fortunately, a mutation in his genes caused the cancer to react to treatment as though it were a lesser cancer, which made the radiation and chemotherapy sessions more productive.

"I know, it's kind of funny when you think about it," Steve said. "It responds to the treatment like it was a grade 2 cancer.

"It makes it easier. It makes life expectancy like

at least fourteen years. It was real helpful to hear. Also, they're coming up with new procedures all the time, so I'm optimistic."

The news gave Steve and Louisa time but didn't do much to improve the immediate situation for the family. Steve still struggles to communicate. Words escape him, and the effort of hunting down the vocabulary that seems to be just on the outskirts of his memory becomes exhausting. Even written communication can be tiring, since it is the mental search for words and not the physical act of speaking that causes the strain. After surgery, Steve wanted to brew but still needed time to recover. Finding help was a problem, but not for the reasons one might expect.

"We've had people out of the woodwork who want to come help him," Louisa said. "It's too many. They all want to help brew, which is great, but it's hard too. It was hard for him to communicate well. His communication has gotten so much better, but in the beginning it was difficult. I had to explain to them that I knew they wanted to help, but it was hard for him to explain how to do it, and he needed to explain how to do it for them to help."

Steve did manage to find a handful of individuals who could come regularly enough that he wouldn't need to constantly give instruction and explain the process. He joins them in the brewery and still brews, but he has his assistants to aid him when he needs it. At the same time, the community found ways to help Steve as best they could.

"People offer rides because I can't drive because I've had a seizure," Steve said. "I can't drive for three months. Everybody stepped up and provided meals and all kinds of things. It's been terrific."

The Gorrills couldn't afford to both miss work, but the community pitched in to help.

"My work situation is really different, and I basically was in a situation where I had to go into work and do my job, and I didn't have time to talk to my coworkers, or want to," Louisa said. "People were feeling really bad and knew that was hard for me, but financially I had to go to work. I couldn't take time off, period. One of my coworkers—when I was down and took the week off for Steve's surgery—he went and talked to people and raised all this money. He handed me an envelope for five hundred dollars. That was great, but it was kind of hard too because it was kind of anonymous and I had no idea who contributed. It's been really incredible. People have been mostly so caring and wanting to help out and do whatever they can."

Stories of communities banding together to help a fallen comrade are touching, but Steve's story isn't quite the same. The community of Whitefield did not band together in the months following Steve's illness; they had banded together long before that. When Steve and Louisa made the decision to focus on serving their local community, they formed a permanent bond with their friends and neighbors. The community's reaction wasn't surprising. It was what was expected, the same thing the Gorrills would do if they were in a position to help.

"It's kind of normal, you know?" Steve said of the whole situation.

Still, the help has been appreciated. For a brewer who changed his entire approach in order to better serve his family and his community—which still comes over for happy hour on Thursdays—it has been a welcome relief to be taken care of like family in return.

"That's where I think a lot of the community part of it has come out. I think that it's kind of become sort of everybody's pitched in and helped," Louisa said. "I don't know. It's great. We've always had this atmosphere with people on this neighborhood and our friends. It's that real, casual, you borrow something from each other, and if you're going in town and someone needs a ride it's, 'Can I have a ride in town?' You watch people's animals when they're away, and it's always kind of been that way.

"I think for Steve, just being able to be here, to walk out and have the brewery there. I don't know. It's great. I think that both Steve and I, we had talked about this recently, 'Where else would we want to live?' I don't think there's anywhere we'd rather live. It's just a great place to be. We're lucky, and he's so lucky that he's got the business right here. Granted, it's harder now for sure for him. We don't really know what the future will bring, it will definitely have to bring some changes, but just to have that core and that sense that he's got something going that you enjoy and it's where you want to be. It's been really nice for him."

Back at Blue Hills, things have changed. Andris still plans his brewing schedule around his son, but it is the younger son, Maris, whose drive to preschool on Tuesdays and Thursdays affects his mornings. Soon, Andris and Alysa's third child, a young girl named Sondeila, will likely be the one dictating how early her brewmaster father wakes up. As for Talis, he still determines his father's brew day as well, but in a different manner.

"His bus drives by the brewery every day at 2:50, and I go out and wave, now the whole busload waves," Andris said.

Brewers aren't unique for loving their families. Parents everywhere make sacrifices for their children in some form or another, often giving up their careers in order to raise their kids. But the outpouring of volunteers at Sheepscot highlights something unique about the brewmaster's family within a community. As Louisa noted, "It's really cool [to] own a brewery." Ever since English and German settlers moved in to the East Coast centuries ago, brewers have been providing for their families by providing one of the most precious items for their community: beer. In that way, the product becomes more than a commodity. It becomes a labor of love.

★ 8 ★

"THERE'S AN UNDERLYING THEME HERE"

THE ATTRACTION TO BREWING

It was a cold night, and a clear one. December 2012 was nearing its end, and the hubbub of the holidays was winding down. Cold rains and snow encouraged Nashville residents to stay inside with their families, but there was a buzz and hum on the wind.

Ahead stood a welcome sight: a big warehouse-style building with a brightly lit façade. Cars packed the small parking lot that cozied up to the side of the building—so much so that the only parking left was along the street. A row of large windows along the front gave a view of the warmly lit interior. A couple dozen people were inside, most had beer in their hands or had glasses on the wooden picnic tables in front of them. A few had food brought in from the gourmet food truck parked outside.

A former carpet and flooring showroom, the building now houses Jackalope Brewing Company. Robyn Virball stood behind the long bar, taking orders and pouring beer for her thirsty patrons—including a good number of regulars. As one of the founding partners of Jackalope, Robyn was in her domain. She was pretty with a big smile and blond hair bobbed around her neck. Robyn manages the front-house operations at the brewery and was a big part of its appeal. She and a friend from college, Bailey Spaulding, created Jackalope as the kind of place that would feel welcoming. They started from the ground up, which included the removal of, ironically, horrible flooring. They painted the walls in earthy dark colors and made sure to incorporate "all the little things," like purse hooks underneath the bar. The goal was the same as it is anywhere—draw customers in and keep them long enough to spend their money.

The taproom was comfortable and full of a wide range of customers. There was the big man with a beard who seems to be at every brewery. He passed around a mini-growler of beer brewed in his kitchen to any of his friends who wanted a sip. A couple in their early forties sat at the end of the bar in what appeared to be crisp, new Christmas sweaters—proof that some traditions just won't go away. Several small families occupied some of the picnic tables. The children played nearby while the adults talked over a couple of pints.

But no warm lighting can match the glow of a fireplace, no table is as comfortable as the living room couch, and no bartender as quick or convenient as your own fridge. On top of that, Jackalope doesn't even sell food. So what exactly drew so many people to the brewery? What madness pulled them out of the comfort of their own homes, through the cold night, and into a brewery on this December night?

It had to be the beer. No matter how much Robyn, Bailey, and Steve Wright—the ownership team's third member—focused their attention to the small details, it was always about the beer. They understand that nobody comes out in order to hang a purse somewhere. They came out because the beer was calling to them—the same way it called to the owners.

There was a time in the later part of the twentieth century when small breweries consistently made variations of the same three beers. There were pale ale, amber, and stout. They may have called them blond ales or porters or perhaps red ale, but they were all basically the same, and today's beer-drinking community would pan most of them. Today, it seems as though every brewery makes an IPA. It has become the measuring stick by which beer drinkers define a brewer. The result has been something of a bitterness arms race where every brewer that praises balance over in-your-face hop presence gets blasted online for not knowing what an IPA should really taste like. This is only fueled by brewers, so many of whom are hopheads themselves, who continue to find new ways to incorporate their favorite ingredient into their beer.

On this particular night in Nashville, Jackalope did not have an IPA on tap. Many nights, in fact, are IPA free in the taproom. (They rotate two different versions through, but only as seasonals twice a year.) Instead, I ordered a Rompo Red Rye and sat down with Steve and Robyn to talk. We would talk about their brewery and how they came to be in their current positions, but first I took an inventory of the beer. So often brewers use a sharp hop bitterness to bring out the spicy qualities of the rye malt that made up the majority of the grain bill. I like this, but the Rompo Red was different. It was smooth and clean. Rather than a crisp bite, it had fluid warmth to it. The spiciness of the malt came through as a hint of cinnamon behind honey on top of toasted bread. It was a pleasant surprise. The hops were present but didn't steal the attention away from the play of the malt. They were only there, it seemed, to lend support and make sure the roasted grains and malted rye all played nicely together.

Steve, Robyn, and I grabbed a table in the corner. Robyn wasn't drinking. She said she had been drinking all afternoon with her family and didn't need any more beer, but Steve sat down with a pint of Rompo Red as well. He wore a tan Jackalope hat and, like Robyn, had a quick smile. Robyn and Bailey joked that they brought Steve into the business so that at least one of the partners could grow a beard. They explained, in very practical terms, why they didn't feel the need to add another IPA to the market.

"The recipe we had for our standard IPA used hops that really weren't available to us last year because we were a new brewery and you have to get hop contracts so far in advance," Steve said. "We used Simcoe and Amarillo [hops] in our base recipe. I think we wanted that recipe, and we figured when we get Simcoe and Amarillo we'll do an IPA—that was our original thought. Well, even as a second-year brewery it's really hard to get those hops."

Rather than rush to market with a beer that would be just another IPA, the partners decided that it would be better to wait. It was a patient tactic that might not work in a different locale, but was perfect for the crowd in Nashville. Tennessee, and the South in general, has a burgeoning beer scene, but it is admittedly behind the curve with regard to trends in the industry. For Jackalope, that meant that an IPA probably wasn't necessary. Instead, they could focus on providing beer that their customers appreciated. Robyn pointed to their Thunder Ann American Pale Ale as an example of a hop-forward beer that fits better with their market.

"With our APA being less hoppy than an IPA, it's more approachable," she said. "We get so many people that come in here and like craft beer but don't like hoppy beers, or are people that don't like craft beers and are scared off by hops. They try some crazy IPA and are scared of craft beer. Our APA is a very approachable beer. My mom loved it, and she doesn't really like beer."

"Approachable" is something of a dirty word in some circles. As soon as beer drinkers across the country began to recognize that there was more to beer than thirty-packs at the grocery store, those places that had known it all along seemed to take on an air of superiority. Some of the older beer bars served as guides and models of how to properly initiate new beer drinkers, but others became snobbish. It was like that young kid in the knit cap and mustache that tells you a certain indie rock band used to be cool, but it sold out when others started to appreciate them. As more beer bars opened, some of them followed suit and kept their noses in the air, but many more found it was easier to gain repeat customers with smiles than smirks. Still, there is a lingering impression that the best place to get beers coincides with the rudest bartenders. And likewise there's the assumption that an approachable beer is somehow less worthy than one that smacks you in the face with intense flavors.

Thunder Ann APA is approachable, and that is a good thing. Unlike the Rompo Red, this beer opens up with a citrus and floral bouquet. The hops are abundantly present, but the bitterness is subtle. Many pale ales, especially ones that claim the moniker American pale ale, start with a bitter backbone achieved by adding hops early in the boil to counteract the natural sweetness of the malt. This bitterness subdues the sweetness enough so that it doesn't overpower the delicate hop flavors. But Thunder Ann is different, since it has a gentle bitterness and a strong burst of hop flavors and aroma that come from adding hops late in the boil. The result is a beer with strong hints of grapefruit juice. It wasn't overly sweet, and not overly bitter. Robyn was right—the best word for it was approachable.

The same was true with the third member of Jackalope's year-round lineup—Bearwalker Maple Brown Ale. A lot of brown ales can taste as though they are lost somewhere between heavy caramel sweetness and weak roasted-coffee flavors. This brown ale didn't fall into that trap. There was a subtle hint of maple syrup to play with the darker malts that gave it almost a burnt-sugar taste. It fit nicely alongside a strong hop presence that kept the experience from becoming cloying. With each beer, it was more of the same. The stout on nitrogen didn't blow the drinker away with intricacies from a year spent in bourbon barrels, but it nonetheless elicited sigh of satisfaction. The pumpkin ale wasn't too reminiscent of Thanksgiving—it wasn't pumpkin pie in a bottle—but it had delicious hints of sweet potatoes to complement a spicy yeast strain. Robyn explained that they "hate pumpkin ales," and wanted to brew one they would enjoy.

When it was time to leave for the evening, I was sad that I lived so far away. I would not go back to Jackalope any time soon but wished that I could. It was the type of place I could go every weekend or in the evening after work. It was the type of place I could take my wife, and she would be glad to spend a portion of the evening in their cozy bar. It was not a place for a ticker, that rare breed of beer geek whose sole purpose in drinking is to try a new beer, cross it off his list, and move on. There was no crossing off of Jackalope; it had a magnetism that pulled its patrons in and kept them.

This attraction is felt by those of us who go to sleep dreaming of the perfect pale ale. But not everyone is like us. Jeremy Tofte, the founder of Thai Me Up, a tiny brewery in Jackson Hole, Wyoming, which made a big splash when it took home three medals—two of them gold—at the 2012 Great American Beer Festival, explained the difference between us and them: "They don't plan vacations around visiting brewpubs." His point was that people like us will find good beer no matter what. If our region doesn't get a hot new release, we will drive a few hundred miles to pick up a case from a region that does. Our friends ask us if there's a good place to drink when they travel out of state because we've traveled out of state specifically to drink. Yet every time we find a new place, it's only new to us—the locals knew about it for years.

• • •

Sometimes, that pull does a lot more than change our vacation plans. In the mid 1990s, a young man in California named Jeff Bagby was working at the YMCA—and was planning to make a career of it. "I guess it was my first professional job, I was over in college, and beer was sort of a hobby, a fun thing," Jeff said. "When I graduated and moved back south, I worked for the YMCA, which I had done for summers for years, and was hoping that I could take on a full-time position there. I ran summer camp programs for them—youth programs. It was a pretty extensive job, and I thought they would have a position requiring someone full-time year-round, and it didn't end up happening that way. I basically went out and needed to find something quick."

Looking for work, Jeff figured he could take his commercial driver's license—something he needed to drive the bus for the YMCA—and turn it into a job. He figured he could do something short-term and return to a career at the YMCA or some place like it. Nearby Stone Brewing Co. needed a truck driver, and Jeff applied.

"I interviewed with Greg Koch, and we got along pretty well. He was pretty psyched that I knew as much about beer as I did. It was 1997, so there was a different landscape [than] we're dealing with these days. There's probably a lot of guys coming out of college that know a shit-ton about beer now. So I drove beer for Stone for a little while, and I spent time talking with Steve Wagner and the brewers at the time when I came back from my route. After driving for three months or so, Steve asked me if I'd like to train as a brewer, so I thought shit yeah. It was kind of a roundabout way. I wasn't looking for it, but it came up."

In a way, Jeff never chose beer, but beer chose him. That he happened to get in early with what would become one of the most influential and successful small breweries in the United States, let alone Southern California, was pretty much a matter of happenstance. But Jeff's story isn't remarkable because of how he got into the beer industry, it's remarkable because of how he influenced the industry once it pulled him in. He moved on from Stone, and even returned briefly to the Y, but got back into beer as a brewer at Pizza Port Solana Beach, a small but popular brewpub north of San Diego. He worked for a while at White Labs, the San Diego yeast cultivators that, along with Wyeast, provide the vast majority of yeast strains for American brewers. He worked briefly for another brewpub in the San Diego area, Oggi's Pizza and Brewing Company, before returning to the Pizza Port chain—this time at the Carlsbad location. Jeff's beers helped define what was becoming known as West Coast style, and the awards started flowing in.

Each year during the Great American Beer Festival, an outsider prize presented by Hop Union LLC, Brewing News Publications, and Three Floyds Brewing Company is often the most coveted. One brewery is crowned the Alpha King during an after-hours celebration—an honor that hints at a brewer's ability to master hops and their all-important alpha acids. Jeff claimed that title three times—more than any other brewer. First in 2005, when he worked at Oggi's, then again in 2010 and 2011, for Pizza Port Carlsbad. Along the way were many other GABF awards, World Beer Cup medals, and countless local recognitions.

Jeff's face won't show up on your television screen as he dips his hands in a bunch of hops to bring to his face and inhale their aroma, but his name is commonly brought up by West Coast brewers as one of the best in the region. He was able to learn from some of the masters and pioneers, such as Stone's Steve Wagner and Pizza Port's Tomme Arthur—himself an Alpha King in 2008 who now operates Lost Abbey and Port Brewing—and it all started because he could drive a truck and liked beer.

"I'm very glad it worked out this way," he said. "I didn't really have any kind of direction as to what I wanted to do with myself back then. I liked the aspect of the job at the YMCA that involved training and employing staff. I liked the dealing with customers and face-to-face interaction. I enjoyed the fun parts of working with kids and going to beaches and waterparks and museums—things like that—but I got interested in the other side of it, the more serious side of it, and I saw it as good experience for down the road. That's all I had for direction out of school.

"Beer was a hobby and nothing that I ever thought of as a potential career. When I did become a brewer at Stone, I didn't think much of it then either. A couple coworkers and I joked about one day owning our own places, but knew we were very far from that. I see it as very fortunate. It ended up bringing me where I am today. I probably wouldn't be doing what I'm doing without starting there and having the foundation for my brewing career."

Beer got its hooks deep inside Jeff. The longer he worked in breweries, even when it still involved heavy lifting, early mornings, cleaning kegs, and squeegeeing floors, the more Jeff became a part of the beer community—and the more beer became a part of his life. After all the years in the industry, he ultimately embraced his station as a master brewer. Brewing was no longer a hobby, and it was more than just a job. Like many in his position, Jeff decided to take full ownership of his creations and start his own brewery.

The pull was finally too much for him to resist.

"I'd say really I thought about it forever, way

back when I was at Stone," Jeff said. "It's always been in the back of my mind. It's always been a dream that was maybe going to be a reality, then maybe three or four years ago it was a strong possibility. Having traveled as much as I have and learned as much as I have, it was kind of like you know, I think I can really do this where I need to go and what I need to do."

In the late fall of 2012, Jeff signed a lease for his new brewery in Oceanside, California. It was a step years in the making, and it came two years after Robyn, Bailey, and Steve all felt the same magnetic pull to open Jackalope Brewing.

Unlike Jeff, the Jackalope trio did not take the slow and steady route toward opening a brewery. They belong to a new wave of brewers and brewery owners that jumped straight to the big show. But the pull was the same.

The story begins at St. Andrew's College in Dublin. Robyn was a student there, and Bailey, a Harvard undergrad, was doing a semester abroad. The two met and became friends and remained in contact even after graduation. Both were from the Northeast—Bailey from Vermont, Robyn from New Hampshire—and both shared the appreciation for beer common with residents of that region. After college, Robyn got a job in sales and marketing; Bailey went to law school in Tennessee.

Both of them hated it.

The plan was simple. Bailey, an experienced home brewer, would do the brewing, and Robyn would handle the front-house business—after all, she was the one with experience in sales and marketing. As is the case with most new breweries, and small businesses in general, things were moving slowly as the two navigated the murky bureaucratic process of building a brewery. But along the way, there was someone to help—Steve. He knew the two as friends first. He knew Bailey through his brother-in-law, a fellow law student. And he appreciated what she and Robyn were planning a whole lot more than what he was doing.

"I was working as a financial advisor and really not liking it," Steve said. ("There's an underlying theme here," Robyn noted.) "I think a lot of what I didn't like about it was that I was selling investments that were like Johnson & Johnson, big companies like FedEx—you're selling those companies as more or less a stockbroker selling those stocks in large companies that are really intangible and at the end of the day I didn't know anything about. Then there was something like a Jackalope, and the localness to it. It's selling something you believe in, and selling something local. At the time they were looking for investors, some of the people they were finding were the same people I couldn't sell stocks to because they wanted to invest in things that were local. For me, I did a one-eighty. I went from financial advising to doing anything I could to help Robyn and Bailey at the time."

Steve helped Bailey and Robyn brew at home and develop new recipes. He helped at the brewery, where the renovation from carpet warehouse to taproom required a lot of labor. He became known as Intern Steve, a moniker that still follows him—even after Bailey and Robyn brought him in as a partner. That intern's spirit would serve him well, as he and his partners were just getting started in an industry that could be cruel in its surprises and slow to dole out financial rewards. And unlike Jeff, who made a steady progression toward owning his brewery, the magnetic attrac-tion to beer pulled the three headfirst into the industry and its complications.

It started with learning to brew on a larger scale—first with a glorified home-brew setup called the SABCO Brew-Magic, then eventually with a more-appropriate fifteen-barrel system built by Pacific Brewing Systems.

"People asked how we learned to brew on the big system," Steve said. "Part of it is when you're installing it, you're figuring out where things go and you kind of learn where things go because you have to. Bailey took some classes at Siebel, but other than that we don't really have a traditional background in brewing. We've talked with a lot of brewers, visited a lot of breweries, and certainly gain inspiration from home brewers."

In part because they worked so diligently, Jackalope began to make money, at least enough to stay on track. Robyn joked about refiguring the budget for the brewery's second year: "This year we have a whole lot of money set aside for building maintenance and repairs," after a tumultuous first year in which they endured unanticipated cooling-unit failures and roof leaks. As nascent brewery owners, they are far less financially secure than in their previous professions. Remarkably, that doesn't seem to bother any of them. They shrugged off the financial adversity with easy smiles and an optimistic patience.

"I think we came here, and we're okay making very little money, but we hope to make money in the long run," Robyn said. "It's a slow burn with the investment, that's the thing. There are other investments that people can make that people will turn their cash around much more quickly. We're okay with things taking a while, but we would like to eventually make money.

"You just have to think logically about how it goes. I think a big problem with breweries is they expand too quickly and you can't fulfill the needs of your base customers. We want to be careful about growing, and when you're careful like that you don't make money too quickly. We can expand super quickly and fast and not have the production to match it, and then you shoot yourself in the foot."

This desire to control the brewery's growth and profit potential for the purpose of taking care of their core customers is a recurring theme. It's why brewery founders like Stone's Greg Koch, Sierra Nevada's Ken Grossman, and Boston Beer Company's Jim Koch still maintain control of their companies when a merger with one of the giants in the industry would have long ago made them wealthier men. Certainly, Steve echoed Robyn's sentiments.

"We're young, there isn't a ton of money like working capital so we can hire a lot of different people," he said. "What we feel is on our side is you can really control the culture of Jackalope really well right now. The only way to keep that culture and control what Jackalope is is to grow more slowly, or organically. We don't have the deep pockets, and so we need to direct the ship by keeping what we do well—which is we have a fun culture. We don't take ourselves too seriously. We appeal to the beer drinkers, but there are a lot of other people who don't know what a good craft beer is, and we want to get those people in here just as much."

For people like the Jackalope trio, it makes sense that they do not fret over making a lot of money very fast. Both Steve and Robyn were in the types of careers that have promising financial futures. Bailey, as a law student, was on a path to financial security. Yet none of them were happy with the chosen path. Clearly, it wasn't the desire for instant rewards that pulled them onto this other direction.

When Jeff's brewpub opens, it has a good chance of being every bit as successful as the emerging Jackalope Brewing. The main reason for that has little to do with the quality of the beer—although it is safe to assume that Jeff's pub will be a top-notch beer destination—and a lot to do with experience. Not only does he have brewing experience, but he also has brewery business experience. Jeff took the long way to brewery ownership, and his company will likely benefit from it.

Although their paths were different, all fledgling brewers face the same risks. Jeff brings along the advantage of experience, while the Jackalope trio are young enough to endure hard moments along the road. The ride is like catching a big wave. Every individual takes his or her own approach. One may go in shouting a battle cry; another may go quietly to appreciate the moment of Zen. Either way, the call of the big wave remains too much to resist, and the only true way to approach it is boldly.

★ 9 ★

"SOMEBODY PLEASE NOTICE WE'RE HERE!"

MAKING BOLD AND AGGRESSIVE DECISIONS

Nebraska Brewing Company? What's the deal with those guys?"

I didn't know the answer to Bill Moore's question. Frankly, I didn't exactly know what it meant. Lancaster Brewing Company's brewmaster had plenty to worry about with his own bustling and ever-expanding brewery nearly twelve hundred miles away from Paul Kavulak's pub in Papillion, Nebraska. Yet there we were, sipping on Moore's signature Hop Hog IPA and talking about Nebraska Brewing Company.

I think what Moore was trying to determine was *why* he knew about Nebraska Brewing Company. Why had he heard about them, and why did they seem to be the subject of so much discussion?

Part of it was the nature of the modern beer community, in which every poster on forums and every beer blogger with a pun-addled Web site can churn out opinions and criticisms with seeming credibility. Paul drew a lot of criticism when his brewpub began distributing outside of Nebraska, and drinkers in farther corners of the country got a look at the brewery's labels. Someone in cyber-space decided that the labels were strikingly similar to those of The Bruery—a popular brewery from Southern California helmed by talented brewer Patrick Rue. Although there are certainly similarities between the two labels, most notably the unique shapes of those of The Bruery and the Inception Series from Nebraska, there are more than enough differences to make them each distinctive.

But just to add fuel to the beer geek's often irrational fire, Paul thought he might have some fun. According to him, he was at a beer festival with Patrick and decided that a little more Internet controversy could be amusing.

"I dealt with quite a few of those threads and finally there was one on *BeerAdvocate*; it was one of our Inception Series beers called Microbe Rue," Paul said. "That thread took off, and by the time I found the thread it was like one hundred lines deep. It was all, 'Nebraska is copying The Bruery.' Patrick Rue and I, I told him we're going to name a beer with the word Rue in the title and it will be this whole flare-up again. We laughed about it."

Flare up it did. Despite the fact that the beer was only made once and just a dozen cases were produced, the collective world of beer geeks seemed convinced that Paul and Nebraska Brewing Company were out to make a profit by imitating The Bruery. Eventually, the thread drew enough attention that Paul replied to it directly—which only drew more attention.

"I responded to the thread, and I did the whole [Dogfish Head founder Sam] Calagione, 'look guys, here's what's going on' thing, and I ended it well and said, 'What matters most is the beer, cheers.' And I left it. I was like, okay, maybe that will put the flames out a bit, and then BeerNews .org took my response and stuck it on *BeerNews* like, 'Nebraska Brewing Company takes them head on,' I was like, 'Oh geez, here we go.'"

There. That was it. That's why we were talking about them in Lancaster. It did not matter so much that Nebraska Brewing Company's labels looked like The Bruery's. It was the way Paul addressed the controversy. The fact that he compared himself to one of the most popular figures in American beer, who similarly chided forum users for their overly critical comments in a post that went viral across the beer community, was not the point. Nor was much of the other stuff that drew rampant criticism from those who delight in such. What mattered was that Paul, in representing his brewery, was willingly putting himself in those discussions—mentioning his own brewery in the same breath as beer geek meccas such as Dogfish Head and luminaries like Rue and Calagione. When conflict arose, he didn't shrink away or shrug it off; he charged toward it and put himself in the center of discussion—daring anyone else to come back at him. It was aggressive.

It turned out that aggression was something of a recurring theme for Nebraska Brewing Company, and it has been a central characteristic of many modern brewers. From the start, the brewery was perceived as having an insistent nature. When it opened in November of 2007, few brewers in the region were pushing the palates of the local customers. But Paul was not content to brew endless amounts of blonde ales, Kölschs, and amber ales because he had been told that he could never sell an IPA in Nebraska: "We had several people from the very beginning tell us not to make those beers," head brewer Tyson Arp said. " 'You're not going to sell them. It's going to be a disaster.' " They brewed them anyway. They stretched the limits of what local drinkers wanted, and when they exceeded those limits, they sought out new markets. They found distributors willing to move their beer beyond the walls of the pub until the locals caught on to just how good it was. Still not confident enough that the local opinions and ever-increasing positive feedback was a true reflection of their product's quality, they entered more and more beer competitions— and they started winning.

At each step along the way in building their market and reputation, Nebraska Brewing

Company was met with criticism and second-guessers on blogs and forums. People told them to their faces that their tactics would not work in Nebraska. Yet they persisted and stayed on their aggressive course.

They aren't alone. As more and more breweries enter the market, there appears to be a growing trend of aggressive marketing and public relations campaigns. Marketing for small breweries has mostly consisted of word-of-mouth advertising, social media campaigns, and the occasional print ads. So many brewers turn to their labels and packaging, where they can tell a story, painting themselves as renegades rebelling against the tyranny of corporate beer while brewing experimental ales using locally sourced herbs and other, more-bizarre ingredients. For some, this approach comes off as little more than a hype-generating ploy, much the same way most consumers scoff at products marketed to teenagers as "Xtreme!" For others, this approach feels genuine. When a handful of small brewers started popping up in New England and on the West Coast, they were true iconoclasts in their contemporary beer culture. Virtually all American beer at the time was light on flavor and alcohol, and beers like Samuel Adams Boston Lager, Sierra Nevada Pale Ale, and Anchor Steam were aggressive compared with their mega-brewer counterparts. It was out of this tradition that breweries like Stone Brewing Co. were born.

Stone's CEO and cofounder Greg Koch lets the world know his intentions loud and clear. The self-described introvert is not shy when it comes to jumping on a bar with a megaphone to rail against the stranglehold that "fizzy, yellow beer" has over the market. The label on their twenty-two-ounce "bomber" bottles (a format common to smaller brewers who have to fight for every inch of shelf space in stores) for their signature Arrogant Bastard Ale proclaims that its drinkers "are not worthy" of the liquid arrogance they are about to imbibe. It simultaneously smacks of elitism and arrogance but welcomes all who want to be worthy to come and join them in their stance. And according to Greg, it's just Stone being Stone.

"Why does Metallica write aggressive music? It's who they are," he said. "We're just kind of being ourselves. We like being expressive. I don't mind calling dumbed-down, lowest-common-denominator approaches in the commodity world to the mat. I feel free to openly comment about the practices in our world that could stand improvement."

Even without the megaphone, Greg is boisterous. On Twitter, he lambastes the bottled-water industry for its fundamentally wasteful nature. He speaks at conferences and colleges on subjects ranging from the environment and conservation efforts to emerging trends in business and entrepreneurship. And he does this all the time.

Between running his company and making numerous appearances, typically the only time he has for interviews is while he makes his commute home or during one of his frequent trips to the airport. Even so, he is seemingly always willing to speak with media outlets, where he does not pull punches about subjects such as "high-processed food—that's killing us, yet it's freely marketed to children, to our schools, to people in 'food deserts' in our communities and actively promoting things that are not good for ourselves, each other, and our society.

"When I call out some of this stuff," he adds, "sometimes people react negatively that I'm trying to take away their freedom or something. I'm just calling out that the beer industry does dumb shit too. It's not good for the industry, it's not good for the public, and it puts a negative light on everything, but some companies do it anyways."

He is just as quick to criticize the fast food industry as he is to rail against beer distributors who "poach" taps away from small breweries by offering bar owners illegal incentives to take the independent brewery's beer off in favor of something from one of the beer giants with a higher profit margin and faster turnover. One thing he isn't willing to take on is another brewery fighting earnestly for the same thing. While beer geeks may get up in arms about a small brewery like Nebraska Brewing Company coming into their local markets, Greg would rather celebrate them for their pioneering spirit than attack their brashness.

"I would say that there is one entity on the planet whose opinion matters for what the Nebraska Brewing Company should be brewing," he said. "Who should be deciding what Nebraska Brewing Company is brewing? That's Nebraska Brewing Company. If you like it, enjoy it and buy it. If you don't, choose something else.

"I always fail to understand why, when we have more and more choices available every day from a wide perspective, why anybody would complain about a different choice. It makes no sense to me. If Nebraska Brewing Company was reducing the choice of other brands of beers, [I'd understand], but Nebraska Brewing Company doesn't have the power to do that. They're not knocking any light beers off the shelf, they're not knocking any high-ABV, fruity-flavored, energy-enhanced beer off the shelf—they're doing that to themselves. So what's somebody got to complain about?"

Yet it seemed that every move Nebraska Brewing Company made was met with complaints. Starting with their choice in name and moving on to their decision to distribute to other states, the brewery faced opposition at every step—and simply kept plodding forward. Like setting off at a full sprint through a dark tunnel, they did not always know what they would encounter, but they knew that any obstacles they met would be taken on with a full head of steam. At each hurdle, more and more people outside of Nebraska started to take notice.

The strange thing about the conversations that people kept having about Nebraska Brewing Company was that it all seemed to be coming from such an unlikely place; namely, Nebraska. Most people outside of the state associate Nebraska with corn, college football, and perhaps miles and miles of flat, tedious highway. The brewery itself is unassuming. Located in the corner of what appears to be a dreary and common strip mall, Nebraska Brewing Company opens up into a bright, spacious brewpub. Stainless steel tanks line the wall behind the stainless steel bar. Barrels full of the brewery's special and award-winning barrel-aged beers rest on racks scattered throughout the pub. It has an undeniably nice and cozy feeling but still gives off the vibe that it might be just another run-of-the-mill, mass-market brewpub looking to cash in on the beer craze. Do not be mistaken, there is nothing run-of-the-mill about the beer.

"Fortunately most people come in the door and try the beer and let the beer speak for itself, rather than the location," said Paul's wife and brewery cofounder Kim Kavulak.

What the beer has to say can be shocking. The first NBC beer I tried was one of its most renowned: Hop God. A cross between a Belgian Tripel and a West Coast IPA, there was something special in the glass in front of me. With the exception of beers like Piraat Ale from Brouwerij Van Steenberege N.V., of Ertvelde, Belgium, Belgian IPAs are often a confused mess. The American versions taste like a collision of the two styles rather than a symbiotic fusion. It's like a DJ taking the music from one popular song and then playing it behind the words to another. Even though the beats match and it's cleverly done, you would still prefer to listen to the originals.

Not so with Piraat, and not so with Hop God. The same way the hops take somewhat of a backseat to the fruity esters and the bitterness only enhances the dry nature of the Tripel in Piraat, the nuances from the Belgian yeast play a secondary role to the hops in true West Coast fashion for Hop God. It's as though a Belgian Tripel went on vacation in the Pacific Northwest and fell in love with some American hops. It was a glowing hazy-yellow beer with a surprisingly creamy body. It was slightly tart in the way that good lemonade is tart, but without the intense sweetness.

This was not the kind of beer that drinkers have come to expect from Nebraska. Who were the people talented enough, and brave enough, to make a beer like this in the middle of America's heartland, where beer's primary function is to wash down hot dogs at a tailgate party or stuffed, still in the can, up the tail end of a roasting chicken? Who were these people brewing these remarkable beers?

I met up with the Kavulaks and Tyson Arp, as well as his wife, Angela, at their pub. Eastern Nebraska had been hit by a big snowstorm overnight, and the sleepy Omaha suburb of Papillion was slowly and tentatively coming to life as roads were cleared off late in the morning. It was the middle of Omaha Beer Week, and busloads of people were being shuttled around from the various area breweries, brewpubs, and beer bars (the beer culture in Omaha proved to be one of the more underrated beer destinations in the United States). One such shuttle had recently departed from Nebraska Brewing Company, and the pub was calm even though it was lunch hour. Paul, Kim, Tyson, Angela, and a couple of the pub's regulars all sat at a big round table near the far end of the bar.

They certainly didn't look aggressive. Paul gave off a fatherly vibe with a round face, short salt-and-pepper hair, and an easy smile. He had an air of confidence about him but never seemed cocky. Tyson sat next to him, and for a second he looked as though he might be the motor behind Nebraska Brewing Company's distinctive brand. He wore a black button-up work shirt and sported a two-tone black and white beard. But any shade of aggression faded as he spoke. He seemed more like the enthusiastic home brewer turned pro that he is. His wife, Angela, sat next to him. Co-owner Kim sat at the far end of the table. Like Paul, Kim had an easy and generous smile, but it was backed by a hard edge. Nobody in the bunch was flashing bold tattoos or wild haircuts. They all appeared to be down-to-earth and good-natured, so where did all the aggression come from?

According to them, it was born out of necessity. Nebraska Brewing Company never set out to be the kind of assertive brewery that put its name, and its beer, in the mouths of so many beer drinkers across the country.

The critics came before Paul poured his first beer. He and Kim had spent months planning their new brewery, securing a location, having their name and logo printed on their glassware. That name was Flatland Brewing Company. It was intended to represent a sort of Nebraskan pride in being, well, flat. However, there was a problem with Flatland—somebody already owned the name. According to Paul, there was a Flatlander's Restaurant and Brewery in Ohio (I could not find an Ohio brewery by that name, but did come across a Flatlander's in Illinois), and he sought out the owner, Russ Sher, to see if he would mind if they shared the name.

"I remember the conversations well, they were never combative, it was just one-on-one," Paul said. "As much as I tried to convince him that people weren't going to confuse us, one day I was on a conference call and he says, 'Paul, what would you do?' And I said, 'I'd make me change my name.' So I resigned myself to 'Okay, Russ, no more angst on your point.' I went back and said, 'What the hell do I do?'"

The Kavulaks had already invested a lot of capital in artwork surrounding the Flatland name and were hesitant to go back and start from scratch. The obvious decision was staring them in their faces: Flatland and Nebraska had the same number of letters, making a transition in the label relatively seamless.

But they were afraid to take that brand. They were concerned that it would be seen as cocky to take their state's name. It was not the only brewery in Nebraska, and they did not want to alienate the Nebraska brewing community. They were afraid that it would put too much pressure on a fledgling enterprise, as their beers would serve as a representation of all beer in the state to any foreign drinkers simply because of their name. Yet it remained the best option, so rather than cave in to their fears and apprehensions, Paul and Kim decided to embrace the challenge and boldly proclaimed themselves to be Nebraska Brewing Company. The response from critics was swift.

"Immediately I hear, that will never sell in Iowa," Paul said. "People will hate you because of Nebraska football. When you think about all the things I deal with in the blogs, that's when it started."

The name thing turned out just fine for the brewery—in large part because of all that it does for the local beer scene. Paul understood that there were only so many people, even in Nebraska, who would have the opportunity to try their beers in the pub. In order to convince the light American adjunct lager crowd that bitterness could be a good thing in beer, he did not settle with simply brewing a fantastic IPA. Instead, Nebraska Brewing threw a beer festival that celebrated all the good beer that was available in state, as well as exciting beers from other regions of the country. Palates began to shift, and customers began to recognize the brewery as a great spot to grab a pint.

"I don't think we ever questioned ourselves on 'Is the pale ale too aggressive for this market?'" Kim said. " 'Is the IPA too aggressive for this market? Is Hop God?' I don't think that was ever a question for us, because from the very beginning we said we were going to make beers that were great beers. We're not going to dumb them down. We're not going to make what we think the masses are going to consume. We're going to brew it—and when I say 'we' I mean [Paul and Tyson]—but that was the vision, to make great beer and people will find it, people will appreciate it. The craft scene here is growing so that people now seek it out, and not just ours but other great brands like that."

The growth and acceptance did not come instantaneously. Change came slowly, as it almost always does, but Paul and Tyson were not content to wait for Nebraska to come around to them. Word-of-mouth reviews at the brewery told them that their beer was anything from great to way too bitter. The feedback was undoubtedly useful, since it was straight from the lips of their customers, but the reality of the situation was that it did not really tell them much about their beer. Curious as to just how good their beer actually was, Tyson and Paul decided to enter some brewing competitions. And strangely, the criticism came once again. They tell the story:

"We just made what we wanted to make," Paul explained. "When we first started entering competitions in 2009, that had everything to do with 'Okay, the people in Nebraska, we love them, but will they appreciate a hard-core, West Coast IPA?' Probably not. So, let's take that West Coast IPA, let's stick it out there where a bunch of beer judges can look at it and give us some feedback. Of course you get the criticism of 'Well, they're medal-seekers.' That's not it."

"That's the craziest criticism we've ever gotten, I think," Tyson said.

" 'You don't care about us, you just want to win medals.' That's crazy," Paul said, imitating his detractors.

Kim chimed in, "Medals are nice though, we don't want to lie."

"But we just love the beers we make," Tyson said, "and we love sharing them with people. We brew them for people. We don't brew them to win medals."

Yet that's exactly what they did. First with Hop God, then eventually with Mélange à Trois—a world-class Belgian-style golden ale aged in chardonnay barrels. We shared a couple bottles of the golden nectar as we sat. The first was brought out cold and was hazy like Hop God but had a distinctly fruity aroma. The presence of the chardonnay was undeniable and provided a tart balance to the rich malt sweetness. Paul was displeased with the cold bottle and insisted that we drink it the way it was meant to be enjoyed— at room temperature. Room temperature on that frigid day was about 65 degrees. This one poured bright and clear. The chill haze, a cloudiness that forms in unfiltered beer when proteins bond together at low temperatures, was not there, and the hops that had been so faint and subtle in the colder bottle suddenly leapt out onto the tongue and in the nose alongside spicy cloves. The beer went from great to incredible. Paul served it to us the way a young man shows off his pretty new girlfriend. *That's not the best picture of her. Here, check her out with her hair down.*

And of course, this beer too was steeped in controversy. After the beer was released and distributed to big beer markets across the country, a move that in itself drew criticism from bloggers and forum users who were unwilling to pay twenty dollars for a bottle from some brewery they'd never heard of in Nebraska, it drew the attention of Sutter Home Winery. The winemaker produces a blend called Ménage à Trois, and it sent Paul a letter from its lawyers informing him that the two names were too similar and that Nebraska Brewing Company would have to change the name. Paul and his team tinkered with it, trying to find a way to appease Sutter Home and its lawyers, but he could not get over it. He loved the name.

Paul, a student of linguistics, loved it because it meant "blend of three," and represented the beer, the wine, and the oak that gave it the layers of nuance that made it so special. Paul understood that the beer deserved its name and that he did not want to part with it. So he did what he had learned to do best—he took care of it himself.

"I got very frustrated, and I cut our attorneys out of the equation," he said. "I called the other counsel, and we were talking back and forth. I got very irritated, and I was so keyed up I was at that moment where I was going to snap and I didn't. I said, 'You know what, this is a ninety-eight-point beer, you've got a seventy-point wine. This might rub off on you.' There was silence on the other end and I thought, okay, game over. They said, 'Yeah, we've considered that.' I thought, oh, there's some traction here. We wound up with a royalty-free license. The real royalty is we have to send them two bottles a year."

It seems likely that as long as Nebraska Brewing Company continues to expand its share of the market, it is going to be met with critics. It has been that way since the beginning. Every time a die-hard fan of The Bruery sees one of that brewery's beers next to one from Nebraska, he or she may take to the Internet and decry those flatlanders for having the audacity to put their beer in similar packaging and at the same price point as his or her favorite beer. Meanwhile, Patrick Rue and Paul Kavulak may just go share a booth in a Denver beer bar during the Great American Beer Festival and laugh over a few glasses of those same beers.

It is hard to predict what will happen to Nebraska Brewing Company as it deals with the slings and arrows of critics in addition to the normal growing pains of owning and operating a brewery. But it seems safe to assume that Paul will continue to address each new challenge as it arrives. When we spoke, he was working with Tyson on a business plan that would involve building a new production facility to churn out higher volumes of beer while simultaneously giving Tyson and the brewing team more room to experiment on the current system in place at the pub. Even in the midst of controversy, Paul was looking at ways to improve his company. In many ways, his ability to deal with the critics and persevere through the challenges has echoes of the early pioneers of modern beer culture.

Sierra Nevada Brewing Company cofounder Ken Grossman did not have to deal with the Internet barbs that Paul has, mostly because he and then-partner Paul Camusi founded the brewery in 1980. Really, the level of criticism was completely different. American beer meant mass-produced and mass-marketed adjunct lagers, and nobody expected a small outfit in Chico, California, that brewed a bottle-conditioned pale ale with copious amounts of whole-cone hops to redefine that beer style for an American audience—least of all Grossman.

"I think I was quoted somewhere as saying probably on a nationwide basis, if we could sell ten thousand barrels of hoppy bottle-conditioned pale ale, I'd be amazed," he said. "I think our expectations of people who would appreciate an almost 40-[IBU] beer that had yeast in it was pretty limited, and that was sort of my view of the world back then."

Sierra Nevada Pale Ale was and still is a bitter

beer. Those forty International Bittering Units were well above the ten to fifteen mark of the industrial lager brewers. Coupled with ample amounts of malt to provide the requisite sweetness to balance out that bitterness, Sierra Nevada was making a bold and aggressive foray into the palates of California consumers. They were not exactly alone, as Fritz Maytag was brewing Anchor Steam in San Francisco and Jack McAuliffe was operating the now-defunct New Albion Brewing Company in Sonoma—both of which served as inspiration for Grossman and Camusi. At Sierra Nevada, they were among the earliest pioneers in the modern beer world. Unlike Nebraska Brewing Company, which had no choice but to grow up under scrutiny from industry insiders and consumers alike, Sierra Nevada was allowed to operate without attack. Instead, Grossman and Camusi were left to their own—admittedly limited—devices.

"I guess to start off we were incredibly naïve. We didn't realize all the challenges we were facing until we started up and got in the middle of it," Grossman said. "Back in about 1978, I started writing a business plan that took my brewing hobby to a small commercial level. I actually got a copy of that; it was pretty naïve about the industry and about business. I had a little bit of business experience running a bike shop, but this was a whole new venture.

"We didn't realize all the costs and troubles and things that snuck into our plans as far as making a profit. Pretty much in our first year of business we realized that we had to grow to survive. We were at about a thousand barrels in 1981, our first full year of production, and it was not enough to make a living, so we started to grow the sales and expand outside of our hometown into the Bay Area and Northern California, then eventually the West Coast and Oregon and Washington. But we had a lot to learn about distribution. We hadn't been in the beer industry, so I didn't understand how the three-tier system worked and how the whole supply chain from brewer to distributor to retailer worked and how to satisfy the needs of those levels of the business."

As unprepared for the business as Ken may have been, beer drinkers were ready for Grossman's product. The iconic pale ale is just one of over a dozen beers produced by Sierra Nevada today, and it has been used as the base standard of American pale ale for so many brewers who followed. But Grossman was not necessarily ready to be the man to bring that product to the country. Success was most assuredly not guaranteed for the young company and its brash founders. The problems they faced were unfamiliar in an industry dominated by large brewers.

"There were really no suppliers that catered to our small-budget, small-brewing needs," Grossman said. "So I went to the junior college and learned how to weld and took refrigeration repair classes and electrical wiring classes. And all of those things were self-taught and skills that we needed to get up and running and stay running on a shoestring budget. We had a lot of needs, and we picked them off one by one. One thing with having such a small budget is it created a lot of resourcefulness on how we ran our business. We innovated a lot, and that sort of stuck with us today."

The early challenges facing Sierra Nevada were daunting. Unlike today's market—where a well-funded brewer can purchase new brewhouse equipment and tanks that accommodate all ranges of capacity or a well-connected brewer can get used equipment from any one of the numerous expanding breweries looking to jettison its old tanks—Grossman had to piece together and modify equipment for his brewery on his own. These were problems that could appear as brick walls in the path of progress. But Grossman ran toward them and discovered he could leap and climb over everything that came his way. The problems did not go away, they just became more approachable.

Quickly, he recognized that if the company were to grow—something that Grossman considered essential to Sierra Nevada's survival—it had to learn at least one lesson from the big boys. His beer had to be good, and it had to be consistently good. That meant building a quality-control laboratory. Once again he found himself forced to think creatively to solve his problem.

"Certainly on the brewing side going from brewing as a home brewer to a commercial brewer involves a lot more diligence on consistency and analytical stuff that we didn't have equipment to measure early on," Grossman said. "We had to be resourceful and scrounge around old breweries to come up with lab equipment. We built our own incubator and had some fairly antiquated oxygen-testing equipment that we got from small breweries and sort of pieced together our first quality-control lab. When we opened we realized if we wanted to stay in business we had to get our product to be fairly consistent and it was an early area of focus we realized we needed to have, and we did."

It would be nice to say that it was the beautiful harmony between hops and malt in the Sierra Nevada Pale Ale that spurred the company's growth from a glorified home-brew setup in Chico to one of America's largest producers of beer (Sierra Nevada was the second-largest brewer of craft beer in 2012, and the seventh-largest brewery overall in the United States), but there was a real chance that few people outside of Chico would never have tasted the beer if not for the hard work and aggressive approach taken by its founders.

Although the specifics were different, Paul Kavulak had to take a similar approach to solving his problem. Like Grossman, Paul needed his business to grow in order to succeed. Before his brewery was able to convince enough people in Nebraska that there were more than three drinkable brands of beer, he had to find ways to expand. He looked at the brick walls ahead of him, and he ran straight at them.

"I think I had doubts every single night between two and five a.m. as to how we were getting the job done," Paul said. "Did we have the right people in place? Were we making the right decisions? Were we communicating and letting people know that we're out there? We said, 'Hey, we've got some pretty good beers here. Even if Nebraska isn't beating our door down to buy everything in the tank every week, we should take the beers someplace where people might appreciate it.' Hence, New York, Massachusetts, Oregon, California, and Wisconsin."

Paul's solution was not to stop pushing the boundaries of what Nebraska consumers were comfortable drinking but to expand the boundaries of his beer's distribution. Knowing the plagued nature of Nebraska Brewing Company, it wasn't surprising that this did not come without controversy.

Before I met Paul, my brother and I were in a U-Haul truck in the middle of a five-day drive. As my brother drove toward Omaha, I read a beer forum post criticizing Nebraska Brewing Company for having the audacity to infiltrate the Boston market with twenty-dollar bottles of beer. I couldn't see the harm in a brewery pushing its boundaries, and I said as much on the message board. I vowed to try the beer myself. Paul posted a reply on the forum, saying he would have a bottle of Hop God waiting for me behind the bar.

The beer was as exciting as I hoped it would be. A pint of Hop God, another of their Cardinal Pale Ale, a delightfully hop-forward pale with a strong citrusy nose, and even a pour of a barrel-aged barleywine that was still maturing in the tanks behind the bar, and I was back on my way.

I was glad we stopped. And ultimately I was glad for the vitriol, because it prompted me—and likely others—to give Nebraska a shot and discover something wonderful.

"Wherever you go and whenever you make notice and mention of, it helps," Paul said. "We sit here every day of the week and scream, 'Somebody please notice we're here!' You become a lightning rod one way or another. When the lightning bolt hits, that means someone paid attention . . . in spite of the fact that some of the comments are negative, it's part of the deal."

★ 10 ★

"WHAT DO YOU THINK, YOU LIKE IT?"

APPRECIATING GOOD BEER

Two brewers walked into a bar.

A man was already seated about midway down on a high chair, and one of the brewers, A. J. Stoll, grabbed the seat next to him. A.J., a couple of his cellar workers, and the other brewer all started checking down the sizable beer list and began a conversation with the bartender who just brought the man at the bar his beer.

The man took a sip, and let out a pleased sigh. He wore ragged blue jeans and a T-shirt, and appeared to be on his lunch break. Or maybe he was just grabbing a beer after a morning spent painting the living room in his house. Either way, he seemed to be very happy with this beer in front of him and the free time to have a drink. He took another one and took a moment to admire the amber liquid in front of him before setting the glass back down on the hardwood.

"What are you drinking there?" A.J. asked.

The man was drinking Hoppy Poppy IPA from Figueroa Mountain Brewing Company. The brewery itself, located in Buellton, California, wasn't too far from this bar in Santa Barbara.

"What do you think, you like it?"

"I love it."

"You know those guys are opening a new taproom here in town soon?"

"Really? That's going to be awesome."

By now the rest of A.J.'s group had put in their orders with the bartender and she looked at A.J. for his.

"I'll have a Racer 5," he said.

Maybe the man next to him wondered why he didn't go for the Hoppy Poppy, but the rest of the group didn't. A.J. drinks plenty of Hoppy Poppy at work as the brewmaster for Figueroa Mountain.

The weather was, not surprisingly, beautiful, and the group decided to take their beers outside to a shady table. A.J. clinked glasses with his neighbor before getting up from his own seat and heading for the patio with a confident grin creeping across his boyish face.

The other brewer in the bar was Kevin Pratt. Kevin doesn't often get the chance to go incognito like A.J. and see how random customers are enjoying their beer. A.J. blends in with the typical crowd of twenty-somethings drinking in Santa Barbara, with his short hair and clean face. Kevin, on the other hand, is old enough to be A.J.'s father, and he carries with him a bookish air that suggests he knows a lot about something before he ever opens his mouth. His closed-mouth grin is simultaneously welcoming and knowing, as though he's waiting politely for you to finish your statement before he offers up his pearls of wisdom.

Physical differences aside, the big difference between Kevin and A.J. is that A.J. brews at a production brewery. Even though visitors to either Figueroa Mountain location could look over a simple chain barrier and see him working amongst the gleaming tanks, most of the brewery's beer is consumed off-site in bars or sold in retail stores.

But Kevin works at a brewpub. When he sits at the bar and orders up one of his own beers, he often gets approached by customers with questions about the beer—usually after a busy bartender has pointed him out.

Kevin brews at night after the Santa Barbara Brewing Company closes. But when the brewing shift ends, the floor is drying, and all the hoses are tucked away, the rest of the pub is just starting to come to life. It isn't uncommon to find Kevin at the bar when Brewco, as the locals call it, opens. Sometimes he sits with a beer, but usually it's a cup of coffee and something from the kitchen. The brief moments of respite are his to enjoy before he goes home, maybe for a nap, and to see how things are going in the front of the house. Lately, it has been a rewarding experience.

"It's always a thrill to have somebody with a glass of my beer in their hand," he said. "It's always gratifying when someone says this is the best beer, or this is the only beer I drink here. I know that that comment goes on in every other pub, and everyone has a point of view, and everyone has a favorite. Maybe that favorite is just for the moment, maybe that favorite is just like team colors, but in any case I never get tired of hearing it.

"How could I get tired of hearing that? We always knew in craft beer we'd have groupies, but what they forgot to tell us was that all the groupies would have beer bellies and facial hair. But they're groupies nonetheless."

But there was a time when few would have claimed to be a Brewco groupie, or even a Brewco fan. After an initial period of success with a talented brewer, the quality of the beer and food steadily declined as that brewer left to start his own brewpub in nearby Goleta.

"They had one really good brewer here who went off and started a pretty famous brewpub not too far away from here," Kevin said. "The medals on the wall right now are his. I have all kinds of respect for his brewing expertise and for his ability to brew. He went off and started his own business, which is the right thing to do when you're that good and you want to be recognized for it. Since then it's gone from really bad to pretty good, very competent brewers, but nothing inspired."

That early brewer was Eric Rose, who opened Hollister Brewing Company along with his father, Marshall. He started his career at Brewco as an assistant but was made the head brewer in less than one year. After six years working on the big copper system in the back of the restaurant, he decided it was time to make a name for himself on his own. He did, and along the way the Santa Barbara Brewing Company name began to decline. The final man in the line of successive brewers stuck around for eight months before packing up his things and leaving without notice. By the time Kevin arrived in May 2010, no beer had been brewed for about two months, and the bar was resorting to selling bottles of beer and relying on liquor sales to keep the business afloat. The brewhouse itself was in a state of disrepair. There was a big problem at Brewco, and the beer was just one facet.

"The ownership had bought into the idea that cheaper, cook-from-frozen foods were going to be more profitable," Kevin said. "They completely bought into the idea that they didn't have to prep or make anything fresh here. The less-skilled people they had, the less they had to pay them, etcetera. Even among cooks there's a world of difference in skill level between minimum wage and just twelve or thirteen dollars an hour. It's a world of difference. They were saving two or three bucks an hour, but the problem was revenue was under two million a year here. We have two hundred and fifty seats, and so that is horrific—especially when you consider how much we pay for our rent.

"Our rent was about twenty thousand dollars a month, and the rest of the overhead. You look at that, and one quarter of your revenue is in your overhead alone. I don't care how much you save on food, you're not going to make a profit, and for a couple years—they didn't. On sheer force of their ability to be frugal in their personal lives and on just this kind of location being almost can't fail, being right in the middle of the party zone, they survived through the worst years of the economic downturn. In 2010 the new chef came on board as an assistant and started turning the food around. Taylor started to really make big changes to the food to bring that up. Revenue was already increasing."

Taylor Melonuk runs the kitchen at Brewco, and he has helped usher in the change between a pub where the chicken fingers and ranch dressing were the best option on the menu to a bona fide restaurant with gourmet pizzas and burgers alongside traditional pub fare.

Kevin, who has kitchen experience of his own, played his own part in convincing ownership that changes were necessary. Brewco stands on a busy corner of State Street in downtown Santa Barbara, and an endless stream of tourists pass by during the summer, while college students and young people crowd the sidewalks at night, hopping from club to club. With ample foot traffic, the brewpub was able to survive lean times, even as the locals barely considered it as a viable place to grab a beer, let alone a full meal. Kevin under-stood that in order for Brewco to be a success again, he would have to win over the local customers.

To him, that meant winning over the people with what he called "veto power." His theory is that every relationship, or even every group of friends, has at least one person with veto power.

"Your wife has the veto power," he told me. "If she doesn't like that place, you aren't going there. If you're going on a date with somebody, if she doesn't want to go, you're not going."

While a group of twenty-two-year-old guys may look at a place like the floundering Brewco with its cheap food, cheap beer, full bar, and big-screen TVs as a good spot to start their night, they would probably have a hard time convincing their girl-friends to meet them there. Similarly, a brewpub full of mostly twenty-two-year-old men becomes less appealing to the single men in the group. And although Kevin hesitates to say that his goal was to make the brewpub more female-friendly, that is probably the simplest way to describe the plan.

Basically, Kevin's idea was to eliminate as many reasons as possible for somebody to veto Brewco as a spot for the night. That means embracing vegetarian and vegan options on the menu as well as burgers and wings. It means making a variety of styles of beer but also having liquor and wine available. And it also means embracing one of the things that Santa Barbara Brewing Company has done well since the first day it opened, which is to show big games on big TVs.

"We're a sports bar. We've adopted that theme because that's a dominant way in which we compete," Kevin said. "It's a very important way in which we compete. We draw a crowd for football. We draw a crowd for playoffs. A lot of it has to do with the consistency of food, the consistency of beer, and the availability of liquor. Those things factor into people's decisions."

The brewhouse inside Santa Barbara Brewing Company looks like something of a relic. Although it is similar in design to many of the two-vessel pub systems built by Premier Stainless that inhabit so many start-up breweries, it is far different in appearance. Unlike the shiny, bright steel tank recently installed at Figueroa Mountain, the mash tun and kettle at Brewco aren't very reflective. These are not the copper vessels glamorized in photos of old-world breweries, but the kind of equipment that has been used and abused by a series of less-than-inspired brewers.

Above, on a catwalk over the back end of the restaurant, stainless steel fermenters loom like stoic guardians over the brewery. Even as they were unsuccessful at protecting the brewhouse from its own masters, they kept their watch and held their fermenting beer well. Behind the bar are a series of stainless steel serving tanks connected with tubes and hoses to the carbon dioxide that pumps the beer from the tall, narrow vessels into the taps. The hum of the glycol chiller that pumps coolant throughout the vessels to maintain proper fermentation and serving temperature is an ever-present reminder that Brewco is a working brewery. These elements were never much of a problem for Kevin, but the same could not be said for the hot side of the process.

His first brew session on the equipment only reached a boil after some finagling that involved pumping some of the wort back into the steam-jacketed mash tun in order to reduce the load on the kettle. After the difficult first run, Kevin got to work refining the in-house system.

"By refinements, I mean there were piles of tubing and the rest of it, and I was right there under all of it," Kevin said. "That's how I met the chef at the time here. I was gutting it, and there was a pile of stainless steel tubing and the rest of it just piling up. Motor parts and all this kind of stuff, and I'm underneath. Taylor walks up and says, 'So, you're the new brewer?' I said, 'Maybe. They made me an offer, but I don't know yet.' He said, 'Huh, well, either this is going to be awesome, or we're going out in flames.'"

In many ways, the story of Santa Barbara Brewing Company mirrors that of small breweries in America in general. At the beginning,* there were some talented brewers turning heads. Eric Rose was the Brewco version of Sam Adams's Jim Koch and Sierra Nevada's Ken Grossman. Beer drinkers began to take note, and soon the idea of grabbing a beer on State Street meant a lot more than ordering from the limited selection available at the myriad clubs and bars of Santa Barbara's party district. Following Eric's departure, there were a parade of brewers, some of whom were good—and others who weren't. About the same time the owners started focusing on profitability over quality. Like the beer drinkers who became disenchanted by the "microbrews" of the '90s that had delightful and quirky labels but mediocre beer, Santa Barbarans abandoned Brewco—leaving only the memory of good times.

---

*Here I'm referring to the late-twentieth-century rebirth of the American beer industry outside of the massive brewing corporations that had come to dominate American beer. Good beer existed in this country long before the "craft" revolution of the twentieth century.

Fortunately, the brewpub survived the darker years of its history. As the beer industry was able to hold on thanks to the quality and perseverance of brands like Sam Adams, Anchor, and Sierra Nevada, Brewco survived because it still carried the words Santa Barbara in its name and had a prime location. By the time Kevin Pratt's first beers started pouring, people slowly began to recognize that the Brewco was back.*

And although his new home is beginning to turn a profit and rehabilitate its image, Kevin is far from satisfied with what he has accomplished. For him, this is just the beginning of the reform.

"It's really going to take, on a generalized brew-pub sense, it really takes three major factors,"

---

*After rebuilding the brewhouse, Kevin Pratt attempted to brew an IPA on the new system. He expected that his tinkering had increased the efficiency of the system but was unaware of just how well he had done. At the end of the mash, he had collected a wort so rich with sugar that it would not have been suitable for an IPA but leant itself well to the much-higher-in-alcohol American barleywine style. He upped the hops dosage and then set it away to mature, adding whisky-soaked oak chips to the tank to give the beer the oak-aged flavor that was exceedingly popular in 2010. He dubbed the barleywine Old Wrecollection, in a nod to its high levels of alcohol, and debuted it at the 2010 Santa Barbara Beer Festival. Even those who were the most skeptical of Brewco had to concede that it was back.

he said. "One is a very consistent marketing program. That includes getting your name out there. You need a brand, and you need to market. You need to get your beer in people's hands. That's prong number one.

"Prong number two is meeting and exceeding expectations when they're here. We're continuing to work on that and work on food quality and consistency. We're constantly honing that and making it better and better all the time. We're working on server training. We're working on bartender awareness. We're working on consistency between bartenders, not so much to make it a corporate experience, but to have something that meets and exceeds expectations. We're fortunate right now that we've had a period of time where people's expectations are lower. We want to raise those expectations. We've already raised those expectations, and we're trying to bring that up.

"Number three is really caring about the state of the craft beer world. Brewpubs, at their heart, are very different than breweries. A brewpub is a brewery-themed restaurant. A brewery is all about the beer and can maintain the focus on the beer and be about nothing but the beer and their own marketing . . . a pub is a much more inclusive experience. Not only is the beer an important part of the experience here, so is the food. So is the general atmosphere, so is the company they're with, so are the people surrounding them. All of these things affect how people perceive how we approach the craft beer market or the liquor market or the bottled-beer market in any way shape or form."

For Kevin, the path to assure Brewco's respectability is long and winding. Even as he treads nearer to his eventual goal, there will always be critics. The best breweries have as many as the bad ones, if only because they are more popular. But the real test always resides in the beer itself. If the quality of the beer remains at a high level, then Kevin has succeeded as a brewer.

IPAs are sometimes considered the cheeseburger of beer making. Every brewer in today's industry is measured by his or her ability to brew an IPA, the way a chef can be measured by his or her ability to cook a cheeseburger. With each, the basic principals are simple. An IPA is characterized by its strong hop presence tempered with sweet malt flavors for balance. A cheeseburger is ground beef and cheese. What sets a good brewer and a good chef apart from the crowd is how they are able to find nuance within those ingredients. The chef who incorporates just the right blend of spices into the patties with the perfect pairing of cheese is lauded, while his or her competitor serving a perfectly tasty but nuance-free burger is passed over again and again. Similarly, the brewer who finds ways to blend hop varieties for that perfect balance of pine in the nose and citrus on the sip receives praise (and repeat customers) over the brewer who crafts a simple, grassy IPA with little depth or complexity.

Brewco's Pacific Pale Ale stands as a testament to Kevin's ability to craft a beer to fit a style and satisfy the customer. As a grand master–level certified judge for the BJCP (Beer Judge Certification Program—the recognized authority on beer styles), Kevin understands that his Pacific Pale Ale skews a bit high, both in bitterness and alcohol, for the traditional style guidelines of pale ale. But that shift is crucial to the beer's success, as today's beer drinkers tend to prefer pale ales that showcase the hops more so than the traditional pale ales did in the past. Sierra Nevada played a big part in the redefining of the American pale ale, and that brewery's flagship beer stands as the standard-bearer for the style today.

Kevin's pale ale could have been classified as an IPA ten years ago but would be chastised by hopheads today if he used the moniker* on his beer because the hops aren't overly aggressive. What they are is present from start to finish. It begins with the pleasant, fruity nose. It moves to the middle, where the flavor slowly gives way to

---

*Kevin jokes about the tendency in brewing to add "IPA" to the end of various styles of beer: "IPA stands for 'Improves Profits Automatically.'"

a semisweet honey-like malt backbone, and it ends with a bitter finish that seems to play with the memories of the citrus and honey that came before.

It is arguably the best at the brewpub, but not the one most closely associated with Santa Barbara Brewing Company. Most of Brewco's fans over the years have come to rate the brewpub based on two beers. The first is the Santa Barbara Blonde, which Kevin actually brews as a crisp and very clean pilsner, and the other is Rincon Red. Before Kevin arrived, Rincon Red had devolved into a complete mess that no longer resembled the well-balanced beer it was supposed to be. There were sweet notes of caramel, but there were also strange flavors from what could have been an overcomplicated malt bill or simply bad fermentation technique. What exactly went wrong with Rincon Red wasn't clear. What was clear, however, was Santa Barbara's gratefulness when Kevin found a way to revive it.

"I was excited by how fast locals figured out there was a new brewer here and came in to check it out and how many compliments I got," Kevin said. "I like making reds, and I think I do them pretty well. Wherever I go, my reds typically become a cult favorite. I kind of make them for what the times are and where I'm at. This current one is the classic Irish red backbone with the hops of a pale ale. It's that simple, but I often find that my best beers are the simplest ones. That was the one beer where I actually got thanked by locals for making it good again. 'You're the brewer? I love this red. Thanks for making it good again.' That first month, I couldn't walk down the bar without getting stopped about that beer."

Kevin says that there are three types of brewers. The first category, the one he places himself in, is the Workman.

"There are the ones who are real dedicated, stay in one place, and end up in ownership or management. They just keep doing what they do and don't listen to critics, don't worry about trends, and don't do anything but make good beer. That's it, that's all they're interested in. They want to sell it, and they want to be profitable. It's a business with all of the efficiencies of that business."

The second is the Rock Star.

"Then you've got the Rock Stars that somehow develop a cult following. Sometimes they want it, sometimes they don't. Sometimes they cultivate it. Oftentimes, they're very inspired and they hit a cord with a certain vocal group of beer aficionados, or the hopperazzis as I like to call them."

The third type is the Contrived Brewer. These are the brewers who release mediocre beer in small batches, but instead of humbly offering up their simple product, they tout it as a unique and rare offering that is made more special by its limited quantities. These brewers may think of themselves as Rock Stars, or they may try to persuade the public as much, but they often fall short. Eventually, after the hype wears off, these brewers fade back into obscurity.

Will Meyers fits firmly into the second category of Kevin's three-tiered system, although he'd probably throw himself into the first. As the brewmaster at Cambridge Brewing Company in Massachusetts, Will has always focused on the beer. Like the Workman brewer, Will has committed many years to the brewpub, which is one of the oldest continually operating brewpubs in the country—and like Sierra Nevada, Anchor Steam, and Sam Adams, one of the few brands that survived the early bubble burst of the late twentieth century.

"Mainly everything that we do, first and foremost, whether it's the beer, whether it's the menu, whether it's an event—the idea is to always make sure that we're doing something that maintains the integrity of our space," Will said. "CBC is a very known entity in the world. It always amazes me how unique a character we've managed to maintain over the years. Plenty of packaging brewers have been able to have great events that they've become known for, but . . . having a restaurant on-site allows us to be a little more versatile, as opposed to bringing in a food truck or catering or something. But really, we want to make this space something special. It's the main reason we haven't branched out to different spots across the country."

Over the course of Will's twenty-year tenure at CBC, the brewpub has maintained its position as a unique and innovative location. Like any restaurant, the little brewpub tucked away in Cambridge's Kendall Square has faced its share of hardships, but it never succumbed to the pressures of a profit-first mentality that nearly undid Santa Barbara Brewing Company and others like it. Perhaps because Will has been on board long enough to build a strong relationship with CBC owner Phil Bannatyne, he was given the freedom to experiment with new styles and techniques. CBC made waves as one of the first American breweries to brew a traditional Bavarian Hefeweizen, with banana and clove aromas and all, but really made a mark as an innovator by experimenting with barrel-aging, adding Brettanomyces,* and secondary fermentations with fruit. The resulting beers stood out from the sea of beers in the market—even

---

*There are several strains of Brettanomyces, but in simple terms it is an unconventional brewing yeast that typically provides "funky" flavors in beer. It is commonly found naturally in used wine barrels (although it is a wholly undesirable spoiler of wine) and is often paired with blends of bacteria like Lactobacillus in the making of sour beers.

as that market grew to incorporate similarly experimental brews.

These beers made Will a Rock Star—a revered figure in the industry with his own set of groupies. Many of them can be seen in CBC's bar, either bellied up to it or on the lifelike mural painted on the wall depicting, among others, Will, Phil, prominent bartenders, and longtime regulars. And as CBC has grown to include a team of brewers, Will and his staff have been given the opportunity to continue their experimentation and innovation. They have so much freedom that perhaps Kevin's system should be expanded to include a fourth type of brewer.

"I personally identify as a brewpub brewer," Will said. "I wouldn't necessarily be happy in a straight-up, production-only setting. But that's more from a creative point of view. From a production standpoint I like the opportunity to be creative instead of just cranking up twenty-five thousand barrels of our IPA."

Creativity is the hallmark of the brewpub brewer. The ability to brew small batches allows a brewer in a brewpub more leeway than one in a production facility. If the resulting product is a disaster, it can always be jettisoned (along with the brewer's tears) down the drain. But more importantly, brewing in a brewpub allows a brewer the chance to figuratively hold their customers' hands as they give the strange new flavors a try. A customer at home might dump a tart, fizzy Berlinner Weisse into the sink, turned off by its strange similarity to sourdough bread, with little resemblance to the beers they normally drink. In a brewpub setting, a server can explain how the Berlinner Weisse, with its low alcohol levels and high acidity, was a traditional breakfast beer when it was first devised. They might add that the style is traditionally offered with wood-ruff syrup for those who want a sweeter beer. Suddenly, the beer has gone from strange to new and exciting for the consumer.

"[In a package brewery,] you're basically putting it out there all by its lonesome with nobody to assist, necessarily, in education and in many cases the necessary hand sell," Will said. "But here at the brewpub, we have a very unique front of the house that is always kept up in the list of what we're doing. They know when something cool is going to come out, and we spend a lot of time, twice a day, with staff training on beer as well as on food."

Kevin and Will are in very different situations. Will has presided over an established location for twenty years, whereas Kevin spent his first years at Brewco attempting to rehabilitate the brewery. And the two brewers are separated by more than the thousands of miles between Santa Barbara and Cambridge. Although Kevin is far from averse to experimentation, he approaches the creation of new beers with the very specific goal of selling those beers on a regular basis. For Kevin, there is no joy in stretching the boundaries of beer and expanding the tastes of his patrons if it means brewing a beer that does not sell well. This does not make him less of a brewer, just a pragmatist. Will, on the other hand, is unafraid of brewing something that might be too advanced or bizarre for the contemporary customer—which is exactly what he has been doing for two decades.

"We've been given the opportunity not only to really hone our craft and really refine craft beer styles and such but also to push the envelope and be extremely creative in situations where other people wouldn't be afforded the opportunity— especially in a packaging brewery," Will said. "We were one of the earliest breweries in the country to do a lot of barrel aging and make some pretty extraordinary beers playing around with fermentation, wild yeast, etcetera. In a brewpub, that's pretty big here. Besides being concerned about cross-contamination, you don't have the packaging-line concerns and the packing issues involved. You don't have the marketing concerns that come along with it either."

The difference between the two brewers is an interesting part of their story, but what they share and where their ideologies converge is the source of their true value. For both, the most important aspects of their job are crafting something that can further the brewpub for which they work and finding ways to put the customer first. As willing as he may be to stretch the boundaries beyond the comfort zones of the typical beer drinker, Will never lets his mind stray too far away from the customer.

The dedication to the patron is evident in the way CBC handles its special events. Kevin's ability to reduce a complex entity such as a brewpub down to a simple description (i.e., a "brewery-themed restaurant") is one of the endearing qualities of the pragmatic brewer, but it also highlights an essential tool at the disposal of the brewpub brewer that is typically unavailable to packaging brewers—the kitchen. CBC makes an effort to ensure that its menu items are locally sourced and sustainable, but the focus remains on the experience of the customer. Even at the somewhat regular brewer's dinners and anniversary parties that change CBC from a top-notch brewpub into a food-and-beer connoisseur's dream setting manage to hold on to a casual atmosphere. As the kitchen staff turns out fine-dining food, the customers comfortably enjoy it as themselves in jeans and T-shirts.

"We're still not comfortable with the white tablecloth, fancy-service idea," Will said. "We're still CBC. Whether we have a particularly extraordinary refined menu for an event or not, we don't think that compromises our standing as a place to have either a really fine meal or some pretty casual nachos or burgers. Our kitchen is extremely versatile. They maintain our focus on locally sourced and agriculturally sustainable produce and protein, but they're able to do really nice things as well as some casual but excellent pub food."

What Kevin and Will are able to do—specifically to have a direct interaction with their customers and to share in that moment of appreciation with them—sets them apart as brewpub brewers. At Blue Hills, when the wort was in the kettle and all that remained were a couple of hop additions, Andris would fire up the patio grill he kept just outside the back door and pour himself a pint of his IPA. After the hot and steamy work of unloading the mash and then later cleaning the mash tun and the grates of the false bottom, he usually enjoyed the ever-so-slightly buttery IPA with an intern or two, as they chomped down on a hot cheeseburger or bratwurst while checking their watches to make sure they added the hops on time.

That moment of enjoyment, even if it was the best part of the day, was only shared by a handful of insiders. Ultimately, Andris could proclaim how fine his beer was as much as he wanted, but if the beer drinkers weren't ordering the IPA at the bar, then he had a problem. In order to gauge the reception of his beers in the market, Andris would check online forums and reviews for his beers, but he would also enact the same routine A. J. Stoll did with the man at the bar in Santa Barbara. A musician himself, the Blue Hills brewmaster frequently visited bars that happened to sell his beer when he went to see friends play. He would loudly and conspicuously head to the bar and order a Blue Hills, usually with a more-heavily inflected Massachusetts accent than usual, and then look around to note the reactions of others at the bar. If others ordered his beer, he would ask them what they thought of it, just as A.J. had done. For the package brewer, especially those working on a smaller scale, this form of undercover market research was the best and only way they were able to get feedback from their customer. Sales numbers were one thing, as were the reviews, but both can be misread. What really mattered was being able to interact with the customer and gain the honest feedback of the most important consumers.

This word-of-mouth litmus test is far simpler for brewpub brewers like Kevin and Will. The chances of either going unrecognized in his own pub are slim—especially at Cambridge Brewing Company, where Will's face is portrayed on one of the brewpub's inner walls—and they are never too far removed from the customer's direct appraisals. When patrons come in and sample a flight of beer, their reactions are visible. If they sit at the bar, their conversations are audible as well.

This direct interaction with the consumer is emerging as a preferred model for new small breweries. Although legal restrictions limit them in many states—Massachusetts, for example, which does not allow the sale of beer for on-site consumption at a brewery*—many new breweries open with a taproom at the facility where customers can buy and drink the beer on site. As A.J. hinted to the man at the bar, Figueroa Mountain opted for the taproom experience with a new location in Santa Barbara. Their Buellton brewery had always had a taproom of its own, but Buellton is a small town, and the brewery received little, if any, foot traffic. With its second location in Santa Barbara's Funk Zone, an industrial district punctuated by murals, art studios, and wineries, A.J. now has a place where he can gain honest feedback from any of the scores of customers who wander in after an afternoon of shopping or volleyball at the beach. To the brewer, there is little in the world more appreciated than watching a stranger order their beer and hearing them say, "That's a damn fine beer."

---

*Of course, brewers have found ways around this restriction. It may bend some rules, but it is not too uncommon to find a brewery that will sell a logo-embossed pint glass and then offer to fill it with a "free sample."

★ EPILOGUE ★

"WE'RE GETTING BIGGER EVERY DAY"

THE FUTURE OF CRAFT BEER

After more than a year away from Blue Hills, I visited the brewery again in December 2011. I was in town to ring in the coming new year with friends but also to check back in with Andris and see how the brewery had grown and where it was heading. I was an assistant there when it was in its infancy. It was a toddler now and beginning to make bigger and bigger steps into the local beer world. Andris was eager to show it off—especially to someone who had seen it in its early days.

"Come on down, you can meet the new crop of interns, and we'll brew a batch together. Actually, it's perfect timing—we're going to be brewing our first Anniversary Ale, which is actually for our second anniversary, but who better to come down and brew it than someone who was around at the beginning?"

I was flattered by the sentiments, even if I knew my impact on the beer would be negligible. Andris would design the beer, perhaps take some input from his assistants, and then it would be up to the whole brewing team to make sure it was carried out properly. I was more excited about the chance to catch up with a friend and share a couple of beers.

I thought about the brewery itself, how much empty space there was, where Andris hoped to install a couple more fermentation tanks. In one corner of the brewery floor, tucked away next to the stack of clean kegs, rested a pallet full of fifty-five-pound bags of grain. When a new delivery arrived, those stacks got to be about four feet tall, never much bigger. The kegs, stacked three high, took up more room than anything else. During my tenure there, another assistant, Eric, always had big ideas for all that extra space.

"You really need to get a bottling line in here, Andris," he would say about once a month—usually as we were busy hand-filling sixty-four-ounce growlers and twenty-two-ounce bottles.

"I'm telling you—we don't have the room. Trust me on this one," Andris replied again and again.

Arriving to Canton from Boston that morning, the brewery suddenly didn't seem so spacious anymore.

Andris was out when I arrived, but the brewery was teeming with activity. Unlike the occasional quiet mornings when I was alone at Blue Hills, there was a hum of constant activity now. The brewery's delivery driver, Scott, was operating a loud gas-engine forklift—carrying a pallet of grain in from the loading dock. The grain was no longer tucked away in a corner. In its place were countless boxes of twenty-two-ounce bottles waiting to be filled. The grain was moved onto a second level of warehouse shelves that jutted out past the small office inside the brewery. The kegs seemed to take up an even bigger portion of the brewery, yet they no longer had the biggest footprint. That belonged to the row of fermentation vessels, which had grown since my last visit by two more twenty-barrel tanks.

In addition to the equipment, the brewery was crowded with more people. The new interns* were Billy and Eric. Billy, who would later take a job running the kegging line at Harpoon Brewery, wore a ball cap, blue jeans, and a large long-sleeve shirt, scrunched halfway up his forearms. His full beard completed the look. Eric, who at the time of this writing had left for brewing school at UC Davis, wore glasses and a goatee. I introduced myself, and they seemed to recognize my name enough to trust me but went about their business as I was left to stand on the sidelines. I offered to help. By the time Andris came in, I was dumping bags of grain into the mash tun.

---

*Andris and his partners must have learned as much from me as I did from them. After I left, Blue Hills started an internship program that gave young brewers an opportunity to practice their brewing skills at an actual production brewery.

"You look like you've done that before," he shouted as he came in. "Hop on down and let me show you around. Billy will finish up, up there."

Billy hopped up to the platform and quickly slashed open a bag of grain with the blade kept on a nearby shelf for that purpose. He tore it open and hoisted the bag to his shoulder with the quick movements of a practiced worker. My last time filling the mash tun at Blue Hills had been going much like my first—which is to say a little too slowly.

Andris briefly showed me around the storage room that he rented out from the unit next door. It was small, but big enough to house the forklift, some supplies, and more kegs. Outside, away from the roar of the boiler and the din of the brewery, Andris and I chatted about how much things had changed.

"We're growing. We're getting bigger every day," he said. "It's getting hard to find the space to put it all. Well, it was always hard, but now it's getting really hard."

He went into details about his current lease and the negotiations with his landlord. Andris was hoping to move in to one of the bigger units in the industrial complex but was facing some resistance. Nobody likes the process of moving, and moving a brewery is especially unsavory work, but it was beginning to look like a real possibility for Blue Hills.

"The problem isn't the floor space. I can get floor space here or next door or whatever," Andris said. "The problem is finding a place with the right ceiling height."

As it was, the fermentation vessels at Blue Hills stood nearly as high as the ceilings. With more floor space, Blue Hills could continue to add extra twenty-barrel tanks, but nothing larger. The real key for a brewery expansion is being able to add larger tanks. The bigger tanks are filled with the brewery's most popular beers, which allow the brewer to focus on seasonals and secondary beers that help establish a brand. It is hard to brew a properly made seasonal beer such as a Marzen, which can take up a tank for six weeks or more as the beer develops the right flavor profile, when those tanks need to be filled with IPA again and again.

"I don't know what I'm going to do if I don't get the space I want," Andris said, "but I'm going to have to do it soon. There's no more room to grow here."

The question of what will happen to the still-young craft beer industry as the market evolves is the subject of constant commentary, speculation, and questions. Columnists, beer writers, beer bloggers, and brewers themselves often seem preoccupied with the notion of what will happen in the near future.

The craft beer segment continues to grow at a fast rate, and although it doesn't come close to matching the brewing heavyweights such as A-B InBev in terms of volume or sales, the growth remains impressive. The one question asked again and again is, How long can it last?

"It can continue to expand, but the survival rate—it can't be one hundred percent," Boston Brewing Company's Jim Koch said. "Of the breweries that were around when I started, there were just a handful, and it's twenty-nine years later, and there's only two that made it. Me and Ken Grossman at Sierra are the only ones from those pre-'85 days that are still there and still running our own breweries. I know the survival rate is not going to be one hundred percent. Don't ask me what it's going to be. Last year, the number of breweries in the U.S. increased by twenty percent. Can that continue for thirty years? I'm just going to do the math. If it did, there would be five hundred seventy thousand breweries in the U.S. I don't think that's going to happen. At some point it will stop and there will be a retrenchment."

Jim didn't use the word "bubble," but he offered a valid assessment of the current growth of American beer. It seems unlikely that the level of growth currently enjoyed by small breweries can continue indefinitely into the future. But the real fear about this newest generation of brewers isn't that the market will no longer sustain new additions or weaker brewers but that all those new additions and weaker brewers might somehow spoil it for the rest of the community.

That was the case in the 1990s, as microbreweries and brewpubs began to emerge as alternatives to the industrial beers that dominated the markets. Breweries like Samuel Adams, Anchor Steam, and Sierra Nevada all fell into this category, but so did scores of poorly operated businesses that spent most of their money on marketing and label design and had little concern for quality control. Soon, beer drinkers retreated from the new wave of microbreweries and huddled around the safe and consistent lagers that they had come to love. Many stuck with Samuel Adams and Sierra Nevada, but other breweries weren't so lucky. Even if a brewery made a quality product, customers were afraid to drink it because they had been disappointed by mediocre beers in bright labels in the past. Small breweries closed their doors, and the days of the microbrewery ended in a whimper.

These are the kind of concerns that faced Jeff Bagby as he was in the planning stages of his first brewery. A brewer like him, who has earned a reputation as a masterful craftsman over the years at various stops—most notably the Pizza Port chain in the San Diego region—would have been at great risk of losing his business during the late-twentieth-century industry shakeout. However, unlike that of the '90s, the contemporary consumer isn't jaded by bad products. A new wave of graduate students may be drowning in student loan debt, but they are also treating themselves to quality beer and food. Brewers have learned from the mistakes of the previous generation, and while mediocre beer certainly exists among the contemporary options, there are enough quality beers—enough breweries like Firestone Walker or Nebraska Brewing Company that have made quality control a top priority—that a bad bottle no longer scares a customer away for good.

"I think about this and how it relates to myself and what we're doing," Jeff said. "To me, it was the right time to do what we're trying to do. More specifically for me to do what I want to do regardless of what the landscape looks like or how many breweries are open and what kind of beers they're making. All of that to me is just that, it's not me. I'm excited for what's going on, I'm excited for what's happening in craft beer. I think a lot of people are talking about is there a bubble, is there not a bubble. To me it doesn't matter. If there is a shakeout or there are breweries that don't make it, I think it's going to be for the same reason there are breweries still open today and some that are closed. There are people that are poorly managing their breweries or making bad decisions or poor-quality beer—it's the same thing that's always happened, there's just more of them in the pool.

"I've really liked the way I've seen craft beer grow in popularity with people that couldn't be bothered in the past, who are really into it and have a foundation for it. I remember when I was in college just walking into liquor stores and seeing a sea of bottles, and it seemed like everybody who could was putting beer in bottle. The quality was all over the place, and it seemed faddish and like it would drop away, and it did. I can remember those days and going to the GABF and finding very poor-quality beer on the floor and wondering how they would make it and survive. I think having seen it happen and been in the industry, I've seen the same thing. Good craft breweries continue to grow and reach new people and change their lineups to make more exciting beer while sticking to their foundation beers. And a lot of new people have come in and been successful, and a lot have come in and not been successful. I think the same thing will continue, and the same reasons places closed or stay open will stay the same.

"I think the crowd that has bought craft beer has grown and will continue to grow," he concluded. "It's been a slow growth. I don't see people turning away from it, and I see more people coming to it. I think hopefully we'll continue to see craft beer grow and probably take a percentage away from the big guys."

The idea that craft beer will continue to grow seems to be universally shared. The reasons for this shared optimism often focus on a shift in what consumers prefer.

"Right now, craft beer really is the only segment of the industry, of the brewing industry anyway, that seems like it's doing well and being well-received," Sierra Nevada's Ken Grossman said. "I think people like to know where their beers come from and that there's people behind them. I think craft has a pretty good-looking future, at least for the next several years. Where it will be ten, twenty, or fifty years from now is hard to say. There's a lot of excitement, growth, and innovation in the U.S. brewing industry right now, and it's pretty much all the small guys."

Ken's Sierra Nevada is among the heavyweights, and it was one of the handful that survived the bubble burst of the late twentieth century. In all likelihood, if the industry sees another collapse that weeds out the weaker brands the way a pride of lions culls a herd of wildebeests, Sierra Nevada will be just fine. Even as it has grown to be the second-largest craft brewery in the country, Ken's company has stuck with the traditions and spirit that made it successful in the first place.

"From our standpoint we really haven't changed

our brewing philosophy," he said. "We still use one hundred percent whole-cone hops. We use all malt. We really haven't changed how we view what we do as brewers at all. We haven't resorted to a lot of money-saving processes and procedures and ingredients as others have. For us, we're going to stick to what we've done and what we like to do."

Sierra Nevada's expansion has been unconventional. Its brewery in Chico, California, was reaching a point of maximum capacity, like Blue Hills'. However, unlike Blue Hills and the numerous small breweries looking to expand, Sierra Nevada was seeing growth in markets all over the country, and not just regionally.

"Our markets have grown significantly over the years and it takes a lot of energy and dollars to ship beer across the country," Ken said. "One of our quality-control measures is to keep beer cold from the warehouse to distribution, as best as we can control that. Doing that cross-country is a big expense."

So Ken and Sierra Nevada decided the best option would be to build a brewery on the East Coast. They weren't alone. Like Sierra Nevada, Colorado-based breweries New Belgium and Oskar Blues also decided to build breweries in or near Asheville, North Carolina. Lagunitas Brewing Company, based in Petaluma, California, is also heading east with a second brewery in Chicago.

"From strictly an environmental footprint side,

having a brewery on the East Coast does help that," Ken said. "We're essentially out of capacity at Chico, so we had to make decisions with either growing the business here or going somewhere else, and it didn't make sense that we would continue to build up the structure at Chico and continue to ship beer across country."

According to a statement by Ken, his son Brian and Stan Cooper will head the operations at the North Carolina facility, establishing the brewery as a family business. However, it does bring up the issue of succession. It seems like a safe bet that Brian will one day replace his father at the helm of the company. Even if he doesn't take over as CEO, one gets the feeling that the Grossman family will remain an influential voice in the company, and that gives us the hope that Sierra Nevada will continue to do business and produce the same kind of quality beer that it has in the past.

At Samuel Adams, the future isn't so certain. So far, Jim has staved off the question with a strategy that has worked fairly well.

"It's hard to predict the future," Jim said. "People ask me what's my succession plan. I have this great succession plan that has worked perfectly for twenty-nine years. I implement it every day. My succession plan is don't die. For twenty-nine years it's worked every single day, so it's pretty good. I have four children. Right now I don't really worry about it, because, frankly, I'm working my ass off. I'm happy doing what I'm doing, so I don't really worry about it that much."

Replacing Jim at Samuel Adams would be a tricky proposition, not only because he is the face and voice behind the company but also because Samuel Adams is a publicly traded company with stockholders to consider. Still, the future remains on Jim's mind.

"I think brewers are very conscious of being sort of the duration of a brewery," he said. "A brewery can exist for centuries. Many have within some enduring structure of ownership—and they're quite different. Carlsberg is owned by a charitable trust and has been for over a century. The Heineken family still controls Heineken. Brewing is unique in that you often have families into their second and third century. Brewers have been very creative and will continue to be creative about ways of perpetuating their values and their legacy. You see that now with New Belgium, where [owner] Kim Jordan was able to monetize, if you will, the fruits of her labor—but instead of selling it to the highest bidder she took a lot of time and did a lot of work to—probably years and years of work—to turn it into an employee-owned company through an ESOP—an employee stock option plan."

The move by Kim to turn the company over to its employees sent ripples through the beer community. It seemed a way to ensure that the brewery maintained its path and stuck to its values. However, it is not the only way the founders of pioneering breweries have decided to end their tenure at the helm of their companies.

In San Francisco, Fritz Maytag took another route. The washing-machine heir and iconic savior of Anchor Brewing (the brewery existed before he purchased it, but he was the one who resurrected the steam beer and turned Anchor into a national brand) was among the earliest pioneers in the American beer renaissance, but by 2010 he was ready to leave the business. He sold his share of the company to a pair of outsiders, Tony Foglio and Keith Greggor. The new owners had a background in the spirits industry and pledged to maintain the brand as a producer of high-quality beer and a staple of the San Francisco community.

Eventually, the feathers that were ruffled by this announcement were smoothed out. Anchor essentially didn't change, and the beer was as delicious as ever. Still, the loss of Fritz Maytag as an active member of the brewing industry was jarring. It was something akin to watching one's father survive a heart attack. Even if the father is able to fully recover and regain an active life, his mortality feels all too real. For the legions of beer fans in America, beer didn't die. However, the optimism that this new wave of breweries would skirt forever the realities and practicalities of the business world did. If Anchor could be sold, so too could the local brewpub. Brewery founders are not immortal, and they could not control their companies forever. This realization was not easy to accept for some.

And just as beer drinkers were adjusting to the news of Anchor's sale and were reassured by the steady consistency of Anchor's beer, the unthinkable happened. About a year after the news of Anchor's sale was reported, it was reported that Chicago-based brewery and pub Goose Island was also selling—to Anheuser-Busch.

If seeing Anchor sold to a pair of good-intentioned businessmen was like watching one's father suffer a heart attack, seeing Goose Island sold to Anheuser-Busch was for many beer drinkers like watching their father pack up his bags and step out for cigarettes. While the sale of Anchor felt alarming because of the uncertainty it caused, both for Anchor itself as well as for the future of other beloved breweries, the sale of Goose Island felt like an absolute betrayal and abandonment. Here was a brewery that had created, and still does, some extremely well-crafted and exciting beers. Variations of its Bourbon County Stout aged in bourbon barrels remain some of the country's most sought-after beers. This brewery that had been among the leaders in terms of reputation, which had already seen founder John Hall's son Greg take over as brewmaster, had apparently decided that the best option for the future of Goose Island was to sell to the world's largest brewing company.

This felt all the more like a betrayal because

Anheuser-Busch had long served as the face of the enemy. When Greg Koch decries the evils of "fizzy yellow lager" and mass-produced corporate beer, his fans think of Bud Light. When brewers tout quality over quantity, beer drinkers recognize the disparity between small-batch brewers and Anheuser-Busch (although in terms of consistency, Budweiser's and Bud Light's are hard to dispute).

It is difficult to speculate on why John Hall, who remained with the company as the CEO, would be willing to sell his brewery to a corporation that had been pegged by so much of the industry as the enemy. In my first conversation with Andris, I asked him what he hoped for his brewery, and his answer surprised me.

"I'd like somebody to offer me ten million dollars for it," he said.

This was completely out of line with what I'd heard from other brewers, who reiterate that they didn't start their breweries in order to make money, but to make good beer. Still, it makes sense. He explained that a payday like that would set him and his children up for life. It also wouldn't stop him from brewing the beer he wanted—it just wouldn't be at Blue Hills.

Goose Island was sold for a reported $38.8 million, which is the kind of money that might change a lot of brewers' minds. Still, the Halls maintained that the reason for the sale was because it was an opportunity for Goose Island to continue its expansion. Not only would a company like Anheuser-Busch have the resources to expand Goose Island's production, but it would also be able to expand Goose Island's distribution. It may have been an unpopular decision, but the sale to Anheuser-Busch was a big boost to the brand, if not the brand image.

Still, many saw the sale of Goose Island as taking the easy way out. They had seen other breweries expand again and again on their own.

"I just want to say, and this is not specific to any one brand, but I can tell you if you've been operating a successful craft brewery for ten years or more, banks are more than happy to do business with you," Stone's Greg Koch said. "No brewery must sell out or has no choice to sell out. If they do sell out, the ownership has decided to sell out for whatever reason. It's fully their right."

Matt Brynildson, who was once Goose Island's head brewer, was among those who shared the initial gut reaction of so many beer lovers. He was stunned by the news. However, his perspective on the situation provided a bit of balance to the debate.

"In all honesty, it's mixed because I had the same gut reaction as a lot of craft beer enthusiasts, like, 'Oh no, one went to the dark side,'" Matt said. "Because I went there and I know the owners—Greg and John Hall worked really hard. They built something amazing and they stepped out at a perfect time, and I think right now they set it up where A-B is still allowing all the craft beers to come out of Fulton Street and the rest of the beers are brewed at other places. I say good for them. They were able to build something and reap the benefits out of it. Hopefully, that doesn't have overwhelming negative impact on the rest of us."

As for Firestone Walker, Matt says that the future is to continue to grow in the steady and slow fashion it already has. But like the rest of us, he's waiting to see what is in store for the industry.

"I think craft will continue to grow," Matt said. "I can't see much further than just a little bit down the road. I hope and I think this generation is solid. Where I think things will start to go funky is when there isn't a new generation to pass the brewery to or there isn't a place for the next generation and these breweries get sold to the big guys and we go back to that consolidation and then breakdown point. Hopefully that's a long ways away."

The sale of Goose Island was a shock to the heart of the brewing world, but it did not signal its death. It wasn't the first time Anheuser-Busch had purchased a stake of a craft company, and it likely won't be the last. With thousands of brewers in the country, it's only a matter of time before others are given the opportunity to sell. It's inevitable, too, that more of the big companies will create brands like Blue Moon, which the Brewers Association labeled as "crafty" because of the way it emulates craft brewers without having the small-business model that most craft breweries are built on.

But ultimately, the sale of Goose Island showed that even though some owners were willing to trade their independence for the security of corporate ownership, others were unwilling to compromise. For every John and Greg Hall, there is a Jim Koch, Ken Grossman, Sam Calagione, and Greg Koch who don't equate getting bigger with abandoning their roots.

"We decide what we do, and people decide how they respond to it," Greg Koch said. "What we do is not just what we brew but how we act and what our standards are. I think if you look back on fifteen years of Stone, coming on sixteen years, and you can see pretty conclusively that we don't change our spot. We're consistent. We're consistent with our attitudes and, frankly, even though we're considered to have a bad attitude, cantankerous and arrogant and all that, when you look at it that's the one percent. Ninety-nine percent of the time we're focused on being inclusive, celebratory, collaborative, sharing our love of the industry, doing great business, and inviting the public into the fold. That's really what we're about."

As owners like Greg Koch continue to steer their companies into the uncertain future, beer drinkers can take solace in the idea that they will hold on to the principles on which they founded their companies. Those values—and those beers —will live on.

ACKNOWLEDGMENTS

This book would not have been possible without the many people who helped me out in some form or another over the course of this project three years in the making. First I must thank my wife, Victoria, for being my first editor and a constant source of support. Thank you. Thank you to my parents, Scott and Karen, and my sister, Kandice, for your encouragement and support. Thanks to my brother, Steve, for driving across the country with me in a U-Haul truck. We suck at driving, but we're pretty good at drinking beer. Thank you to all of the brewers whose voices make this book what it is. Thank you to Andris Veidis, for introducing me to the world of commercial brewing. Thank you to Jim Koch, Ken Grossman, Greg Koch, Mitch Steele, Matt Cole, Rich Norgrove, Paul and Kim Kavulak, Tyson and Angela Arp, Damien Malfara, Matt Keasey, Bill Moore, Jeff Young, Jason Malone, John Obert, John Obert, Jr., Matt Brynildson, Jeff Bagby, Robyn Virball, Steve Wright, Will Meyers, Kevin Pratt, A. J. Stoll, and Steve and Louisa Gorrill. Thank you to Todd and Jason Alström. You guys gave me my first opportunity to write about beer, and it changed my life. Thank you to friends Jim Lallas and Mark Resnick for your early support. Thank you to my agent, Ethan Bassoff, for all of your hard work. Thank you to St. Martin's Press and my editor, Yaniv Soha, for giving me this chance. And a big thank-you to anybody who read this book. I hope you had a few good beers along the way.

BREWERIES CITED IN THIS BOOK

10 Barrel Brewing Company
62970 NE 18th St ★ Bend, OR
(541) 585-1007 ★ 10barrel.com
@10BarrelBrewing

Allagash Brewing Company
50 Industrial Way ★ Portland, ME
(800) 330-5385 ★ allagash.com
@AllagashBrewing

Bear Republic Brewing Company
345 Healdsburg Ave ★ Healdsburg, CA
(707) 433-2337 ★ bearrepublic.com
@brbcbrew

Bend Brewing Co.
1019 NW Brooks St ★ Bend, OR
(541) 383-1599 ★ bendbrewingco.com

Black Star Co-op & Brewery
7020 Easy Wind Dr #100 ★ Austin, TX
(512) 452-2337 ★ blackstar.coop
@blackstarcoop

Blue Hills Brewing Company
1020 Turnpike St ★ Canton, MA
(781) 821-2337 ★ bluehillsbrewery.com
@BHBCanton

Boneyard Beer
37 NW Lake Pl ★ Bend, OR
(541) 323-2325 ★ boneyardbeer.com
@BoneyardBeer

Cambridge Brewing Company
1 Kendall Square #100 ★ Cambridge, MA
(617) 494-1994 ★ cambrew.com
@CambridgeBrewer

Deschutes Brewery
901 SW Simpson Ave ★ Bend, OR
(541) 385-8606 ★ deschutesbrewery.com
@DeschutesBeer

Good People Brewing Company
114 14th St S ★ Birmingham, AL
(205) 286-2337 ★ goodpeoplebrewing.com
@GPBrewing

Fat Head's Brewery
18741 Sheldon Rd ★ Middleburg Heights, OH
(216) 898-0242 ★ fatheadscleveland.com
@FatHeadsBeer

Firestone Walker Brewing Company
1400 Ramada Dr ★ Paso Robles, CA
(805) 225-5911 ★ firestonebeer.com
@FirestoneWalker

Figueroa Mountain Brewing Company
45 Industrial Way ★ Buellton, CA
(805) 694-2252 ★ figmtnbrew.com
@Figmtn

Hollister Brewing Company
6980 Marketplace Dr ★ Goleta, CA
(805) 968-2810 ★ hollisterbrewco.com
@Hollisterbrewco

Jackalope Brewing Company
701 8th Ave S ★ Nashville, TN
(615) 873-4313 ★ jackalopebrew.com
@JackalopeBrew

Lancaster Brewing Company
302 N Plum St ★ Lancaster, PA
(717) 391-6258 ★ lancasterbrewing.com
@LancasterBrew

Mayflower Brewing
12 Resnik Rd ★ Plymouth, MA
(508) 746-2674 ★ mayflowerbrewing.com
@MayflowerBrew

Nebraska Brewing Company
7474 Towne Center Pkwy #101 ★ Papillion, NE
(402) 934-7100 ★ nebraskabrewingco.com
@NEBrewingCo

Old Forge Brewing Company
282 Mill St ★ Danville, PA
(570) 275-8151 ★ oldforgebrewingcompany.com
@Old_Forge_Brew

Russian River Brewing Co.
725 4th St ★ Santa Rosa, CA
(707) 545-2337 ★ russianriverbrewing.com
@RussianRiverBC

Samuel Adams
30 Germania St ★ Boston, MA
(617) 368-5080 ★ samueladams.com
@SamuelAdamsBeer

Santa Barbara Brewing Company
501 State St ★ Santa Barbara, CA
(805) 730-1040 ★ sbbrewco.com
@SBBREWCO

Sheepscot Valley Brewing Company
74 Hollywood Blvd ★ Whitefield, ME
sheepscotbrewing.com

Sierra Nevada Brewing
1075 E 20th St ★ Chico, CA
(530) 893-3520 ★ sierranevada.com
@SierraNevada

Spring House Brewing Co.
25 W King St ★ Lancaster, PA
(717) 399-4009 ★ springhousebeer.com
@SpringHouseBeer

St. Boniface Craft Brewing Company
1701 W Main St ★ Ephrata, PA
(717) 466-6900 ★ @StBonifaceBrew

Stone Brewing Co.
1999 Citracado Pkwy ★ Escondido, CA
(760) 471-4999 ★ stonebrewing.com
@StoneBrewingCo

Stoudt's Brewing Company
2800 N Reading Rd ★ Adamstown, PA
(717) 484-4386 ★ stoudtsbeer.com
@StoudtsBrewery

Telegraph Brewing Company
418 N Salsipuedes St ★ Santa Barbara, CA
(805) 963-5018 ★ telegraphbrewing.com
@TelegraphBrew

The Brew Kettle
8377 Pearl Rd ★ Strongsville, OH
(440) 239-8788 ★ thebrewkettle.com
@BrewKettle

Union Barrel Works
6 N Reamstown Rd ★ Reamstown, PA
(717) 335-7837 ★ unionbarrelworks.com

APPENDIX:
THE BREWING PROCESS

The brewing process differs based on each brewery's equipment, but the fundamentals are essentially the same throughout the industry. Malted barley and other grains are soaked in hot water, in a process known as mashing. During this time, naturally present enzymes in the grain convert complex starches into simpler sugars. Next, the sugary liquid is recirculated over the grain bed, which acts as a natural filter, and then transferred to the brew kettle.

Once the sugary runoff is boiling in the kettle, hops are added for bitterness, flavor, and aroma. Generally, the liquid, now called wort, is boiled for about an hour to seventy-five minutes. It is cooled by being passed through a heat exchanger and then pumped into a fermentation vessel, where yeast is added. The yeast converts the sugar into alcohol and carbon dioxide, in a process known as fermentation. Typically, this process takes place for one or more weeks, depending on the style. Next, some brewers will filter certain beer styles, or it will be packaged in cans, bottles, kegs, or serving tanks and sent to the consumer.

GLOSSARY

Barrel: 1) A wooden vessel used to age or ferment beer or other alcoholic beverages; typically made of oak. 2) A unit of measurement used by the brewing industry; one barrel is equal to thirty-one gallons.

Brettanomyces: A strain of yeast used to add a "funky" characteristic to beer.

Brewhouse: A general term for the working part of the brewery; specifically, the brew kettle as well as the mash and lauter tuns.

Dry-Hop: A process of adding hops to fermenting beer to increase hop aroma.

Hops: The flower of hop bines used to flavor and preserve beer. Hops add bitterness to beer when added to boiling wort and can add floral, herbal, grassy, or fruity aromas to beer when added later.

Hot Liquor Tank: A vessel that provides hot water, known as liquor or brewer's liquor, for the brewhouse. Most importantly, it provides liquor for the mash and sparge.

Lauter: The process of separating clear runoff from the grain bed to transfer it to the brew kettle. This process includes sparging.

Lauter Tun: The vessel where the lauter process takes place; often, it is combined with the mash tun.

Malt: A term used to describe malted barley or other grains that have undergone the malting process, which involves heating the grains and allowing germination to begin. This process encourages the production of enzymes in barley, which is essential to the conversion of starch to sugar in the mash. Maltsters are responsible for malting barley and create various flavors and colors of malt by adjusting the temperature and time of the malting process.

Mash: The process of steeping malted barley and other ingredients in hot water to convert complex starches into simpler sugars capable of being converted into alcohol and carbon dioxide by yeast.

Mash Tun: The vessel where the mash rests. Typically it contains a false bottom, or a metal grate that allows the runoff to be extracted from the mash while leaving the grains in the vessel. It may also include motorized rakes to stir the mash, although many smaller brewers stir the mash by hand with a tool known as a mash paddle. Often, the mash tun is combined with the lauter tun.

Runoff: The sugary liquid extracted from the mash and added to the brew kettle, where it is boiled and hops are added.

Sparge: The process of sprinkling hot water over the grains in the mash to ensure that as much sugar as possible is extracted from them.

Vorlauf: The process of recirculating runoff from the mash back through the grain bed. This process helps ensure maximum sugar extraction from the grain and clarifies the runoff, since the grain bed acts as a natural filter.

Wort: Unfermented beer. Wort is chilled to fermentation temperature, and yeast is added to it to create beer.

Center Point Large Print
600 Brooks Road / PO Box 1
Thorndike, ME 04986-0001 USA

(207) 568-3717

US & Canada:
1 800 929-9108
www.centerpointlargeprint.com